The Wisdom of the East Series

东方智慧丛书

Editors-in-Chief: Tang Wenhui　Liu Zhiqiang

主编：汤文辉　刘志强

Academic Adviser: Zhang Baoquan

学术顾问：张葆全

Chinese-English

汉 英 对 照

Book of Rituals (Selections)

———————— • ————————

礼 记 选 译

Edited and Commented by Zhang Baoquan

选释：张葆全

Translated by Wu Siyuan

翻译：吴思远

Illustrated by Guan Tingyue　Yin Hong　Yang Yang

绘图：关婷月　尹红　杨阳

· 桂林 Guilin ·

GUANGXI NORMAL UNIVERSITY PRESS

广西师范大学出版社

图书在版编目（CIP）数据

礼记选译：汉英对照 / 张葆全选释；吴思远译；关婷月，尹红，杨阳绘. —桂林：广西师范大学出版社，2019.7
（东方智慧丛书 / 汤文辉等主编）
ISBN 978-7-5598-1804-1

Ⅰ . ①礼… Ⅱ . ①张… ②吴… ③关… ④尹… ⑤杨… Ⅲ . ①礼仪－中国－古代②《礼记》－译文－汉、英 Ⅳ . ①K892.9

中国版本图书馆 CIP 数据核字（2019）第 100193 号

广西师范大学出版社出版发行

（广西桂林市五里店路 9 号　邮政编码：541004）
网址：http://www.bbtpress.com
出版人：张艺兵
全国新华书店经销
广西广大印务有限责任公司印刷
（桂林市临桂区秧塘工业园西城大道北侧广西师范大学出版社集团
有限公司创意产业园内　邮政编码：541199）
开本：880 mm × 1 240 mm　1/32
印张：9.5　　字数：197 千字　　图：32 幅
2019 年 7 月第 1 版　　2019 年 7 月第 1 次印刷
定价：78.00 元

如发现印装质量问题，影响阅读，请与出版社发行部门联系调换。

总　序

　　文化交流对人类社会的存在与发展至关重要。季羡林先生曾指出，文化交流是推动人类社会前进的主要动力之一，文化一旦产生，就必然交流，这种交流是任何力量也阻挡不住的。由于文化交流，世界各民族的文化才能互相补充，共同发展，才能形成今天世界上万紫千红的文化繁荣现象。[1]

　　中国与东盟国家的文化交流亦然，并且具有得天独厚的优势。首先，中国与东盟许多国家地理相接，山水相连，不少民族之间普遍存在着跨居、通婚现象，这为文化交流奠定了良好的地理与人文基础。其次，古代中国与世界其他国家建立起的"海上丝绸之路"为中国与东盟国家的经济、文化交流创造了有利的交通条件。

　　中国与东盟诸多使用不同语言文字的民族进行思想与文化对话，

---

[1]季羡林：《文化的冲突与融合·序》，载张岱年、汤一介等《文化的冲突与融合》，北京大学出版社，1997年，第2页。

自然离不开翻译。翻译活动一般又分为口译和笔译两类。有史记载的中国与东盟之间的口译活动可以追溯至西周时期，但笔译活动则出现在明代，至今已逾五百年的历史。

在过去五百年的历史长河中，东盟国家大量地译介了中国的文化作品，其中不少已经融入到本国的文化中去。中国译介东盟国家的作品也不在少数。以文字为载体的相互译介活动，更利于文化的传承与发展，把中国与东盟国家的文化交流推上了更高的层次。

2013年9月，国务院总理李克强在广西南宁举行的第十届中国—东盟博览会开幕式上发表主旨演讲时指出，中国与东盟携手开创了合作的"黄金十年"。他呼吁中国与东盟百尺竿头更进一步，创造新的"钻石十年"。2013年10月，习近平总书记在周边外交工作座谈会上强调要对外介绍好我国的内外方针政策，讲好中国故事，传播好中国声音，把中国梦同周边各国人民过上美好生活的愿望、同地区发展前景对接起来，让命运共同体意识在周边国家落地生根。于是，把中华文化的经典译介至东盟国家，不仅具有重要的历史意义，同时还蕴含着浓厚的时代气息。

所谓交流，自然包括"迎来送往"，《礼记》有言："往而不来，非礼也；来而不往，亦非礼也。"中国与东盟国家一样，既翻译和引进外国的优秀文化，同时也把本国文化的精髓部分推介出去。作为中国最具人文思想的出版社之一——广西师范大学出版社构想了《东方智慧丛书》，并付诸实践，不仅是中国翻译学界、人文学界的大事，更是中国与东盟进行良好沟通、增进相互了解的必然选择。广东外语外贸大学和广西民族大学作为翻译工作的主要承担方，都是国家外语非通用语种本科人才培养基地，拥有东盟语言文字的翻译优势。三个单位的合作将能够擦出更多的火花，向东盟国家更好地传播中华文化。

联合国教科文组织的官员认为，"文化交流是新的全球化现象"。[1]
我们希望顺应这一历史潮流与时代趋势，做一点力所能及的事。

是为序。

刘志强

2015 年 1 月 25 日

---

[1]《联合国教科文组织文化政策与跨文化对话司司长卡特瑞娜·斯泰诺的致辞》，载《世界文化的东亚视角》，北京大学出版社，2004年，第3页。

Preface to The Wisdom of the East Series

Cultural exchanges are of significant importance to the existence and development of human society. Mr. Ji Xianlin once pointed out that cultural exchange was one of the major driving forces for the progress of human society. It is inevitable that communications and exchanges will occur among different cultures. As a result, the interaction and mutual enrichment of cultures contribute to the formation of a diversified world featured by cultural prosperity.[1]

The cultural exchange between China and ASEAN countries, in the trend of mutual communication and interaction, also boasts of its own unique strengths. First of all, China borders many ASEAN countries both by land and by sea, and intermarriage and transnational settlement are common, all of which lay a solid foundation for cultural exchanges. In addition, the "Maritime Silk

---

[1] Ji Xianlin, "Preface to Cultural Conflicts and Integration", in *Cultural Conflicts and Integration*, edited by Zhang Dainian, Tang Yijie, et al. Beijing: Beijing University Press, 1997, p.2.

Road" developed by ancient China and other countries has helped pave the way to a smooth economic and cultural exchange between China and ASEAN countries.

People from China and ASEAN countries use different languages. Thus, to conduct a successful dialogue in the cultural field requires the involvement of translation and oral interpretation. Historical records show that the oral interpretation among people of China and ASEAN can be dated back to the Western Zhou Dynasty (1122-771 B.C.). It is also known that translation started to boom in the Ming Dynasty, which was five hundred years ago.

In the past five hundred years, a large number of Chinese cultural works were translated into many languages of ASEAN countries and many of them have been integrated into their local cultures. China has also translated a lot of works of ASEAN countries. Translation is beneficial to inheritance and development of culture and upgrades the cultural exchanges between China and ASEAN to a higher level.

As Mr. Li Keqiang, Premier of the State Council of the People's Republic of China, pointed out in his speech at the opening ceremony of the 10th China-ASEAN Expo held in Nanning in September, 2013, China and ASEAN jointly created "10 golden years" of cooperation. And he called on both sides to upgrade their cooperation to a new level by creating "10 diamond years". In October, 2013, General Secretary Xi Jinping emphasized, in a meeting with Chinese diplomats, the importance of introducing China's domestic and foreign policies to other countries and regions, and making Chinese voice heard in the world. Xi also pointed out that "Chinese Dream" should be connected with her neighboring countries' dream of a better life and with the development prospect of those countries so as to build up a community of shared destiny. Against such a backdrop, it's of both historical and current significance to translate Chinese classics and introduce them to ASEAN countries.

Exchanges are reciprocal. According to *The Book of Rites*, behaviors that do not reciprocate are not consistent with rites. Like ASEAN countries, China has had excellent foreign cultural works translated and introduced domestically, and also translate and introduce to the outside world the essence of local culture and thoughts. Guangxi Normal University Press, one of the top presses in China that focus on enhancing the influence of the humanities, made the decision to publish *The Wisdom of the East Series*. It is not only a big event in Chinese academia, but also a necessary choice for China and ASEAN to communicate with each other and enhance mutual understanding. Guangdong University of Foreign Studies, and Guangxi University for Nationalities, the main undertakers of the translation project, are both national non-universal languages training bases for undergraduates and boast strengths of ASEAN languages. Cooperation between the two universities and the press will surely facilitate dissemination of traditional Chinese culture to ASEAN countries.

UNESCO officials hold the belief that cultural exchange is a new phenomenon of globalization.[1] We hope that our efforts could breathe the spirit of this historical momentum and help ASEAN countries understand Chinese culture better.

Liu Zhiqiang

January 25, 2015

---

[1] "Speech of Katerina stenou, Director of Division of Cultural Policies and Intercultural Dialogue", from *East Asia's View on World Culture*. Beijing: Beijing University Press, 2004, p.3.

礼记选译
Book of Rituals (Selections)

前　言

古代中国，有十三部书，历经两千多年，一直流传到今天，被人们称为经典（宋代编成《十三经》），视为中国传统文化的源头，《礼记》是其中的一部。

西周初年，周公制礼作乐，当时出现了一部书，原称《礼》（汉代人称为《士礼》，又称《礼经》，晋代改称《仪礼》，今存17篇），全是礼仪的详细记录。

经过数百年，到了春秋末年，孔子创办私学，曾用《诗》《书》《易》《礼》《乐》《春秋》这些经书来教授弟子。战国至西汉初年，儒生们为了解释《礼经》，阐明古礼，纷纷撰写文章，作为读经的参考资料，并用来讲学授徒。后来西汉戴圣将这数百篇十分散乱的文章加以辑录整理，编成一书，共四十九篇，供士人阅读，这就是流传至今的《礼记》。

今本《礼记》四十九篇，有的专释《仪礼》，共21篇，如《冠义》《昏义》等；有的阐发古礼，共13篇，如《王制》《月令》等；有的杂记孔子及弟子言论，共8篇，如《仲尼燕居》《孔子闲居》《檀弓》

等；有的则是极具学术价值的专论，共7篇，如《礼运》《经解》《乐记》《大学》《中庸》《学记》等。

《礼记》的内容十分丰富，仅就思想观点来说，就涉及政治观、社会观、人生观、伦理观、教育观、文艺观等许多方面，而对这些思想观点的阐述，多是围绕一个"礼"字展开的。

在今天，对我们来说，"礼"有什么意义和价值呢？

古人所说的"礼"，含义比今人所说的宽泛。其含义大约有四：（一）礼制，指全社会的等级制度和伦理秩序。（二）礼仪，指具体的礼节仪式。（三）礼俗，指与礼有关的社会习俗。（四）礼貌，指个人在待人接物时所表现出来的道德修养（如恭敬、和顺、谦让等）。

四个含义中"礼制"是主要的。"礼制"是"礼"的核心内容。可以这样说，古人所说的"礼"，其内容主要是指反映尊卑上下的等级制度和秩序。

人类社会的发展，曾经有过漫长的蒙昧时代和野蛮时代。后来由于生产发展了，开始出现了私有制，出现了一夫一妻制的家庭，出现了国家，也就是出现了全社会的等级制度和伦理秩序，于是，文明时代就到来了。

因此可以这样说，"礼"是人类社会发展的产物，它随私有制而产生，也随文明而产生。"礼"是文明的标志，也是文明的开始。它会随着文明社会的发展而不断向前发展。未来更高阶段的礼，必然会适应更高阶段的文明，而更能为所有的人自觉遵守。

古代所出现过的礼制（包含制度和秩序），都是在人类社会发展历史一定阶段上产生，有鲜明的时代特征，即有"个性"。但每一时代的礼制，又都是文明发展史上的一个环节、一层阶梯，较之前代，有所损益，既有所吸取，也有所创新，并给后世留下有用的东西，即有"共性"。这种历史的"积淀"，往往超出时代的局限，而具有全人类的内容。

我们今天对待古代的礼制，既不能全盘肯定，以致抱残守缺，甚至是古非今；也不能全盘否定，割断历史，抛弃传统。正确的态度应是实事求是，从实际出发，抛弃已经"过时"的东西，吸取在今天还有用的东西，继承优秀传统，不断改革和创新。

礼仪，指礼节和仪式，与礼制有着密切的联系。在人际交往和社会生活中，礼仪虽表现为外在的形式，但却包含着深刻的内容和实质，这就是制度和秩序。

据《周礼·大宗伯》记载，当时的"礼"有祭礼（祭天地、祖先、山川）、凶礼（丧葬、哀悼）、宾礼（朝觐、聘问、会盟）、军礼（战事、田猎）、嘉礼（婚冠、饮食、宾射、飨宴）五大类和数十小类。所有的"礼"都有等级规定。各种不同等级的人，在都城、宫室、车旗、服饰、器皿、坐位、用乐、揖让等方面，都有不同的具体要求。周公制礼作乐，使古代中国成为高度文明的礼仪大邦。

周公之后五百年，孔子创立了儒家学派。孔子对周公之"礼"既有继承，又有改造。孔子用"仁"改造了"礼"。作为等级制度和秩序，"礼"原是外在的约束人的制度和秩序，但孔子用"仁"对"礼"做了新的解释，把它转化为内在的自觉的心理欲求。他要求人们克制自己的欲望，言行举止都回到"礼"的轨道上来。他又认为"礼"应以持守中道与和谐为可贵。在等级森严的制度和秩序中，相对待的双方都要以仁爱之心对待对方，在受"礼"的约束上，双方都有责任和义务。具体地说，他提倡君礼臣忠，上宽下敬，父慈子孝，兄友弟恭，夫和妻顺，尊老爱幼，朋友有信，富不骄贫不谄，等等。针对传统礼仪的繁琐，孔子认为各种礼仪都应当从简，重要的不是外在的形式，而是内心的真诚。经过孔子的改造，"礼制"和"礼仪"就更具人文精神，在文明发展史上又上了一个新台阶。

孔子又认为，周公制礼作乐，礼乐是相互为用的，互补的，因而往往礼乐并提。后世儒家的礼乐观，最能体现孔子礼学的本质与孔子的中和思想。儒家认为，制度化的"礼"与精神性的"和"（音乐体现了天地的和谐），两者刚柔相济，不可或缺。礼乐文明一面要注重内心的和平，也就是相同相亲；一面要注重外在的秩序，也就是相异相敬。完全的人格和理想的社会，必须兼具"礼"与"和"之美德，才算是尽善尽美。

礼乐的具体内容当然会随着时代的发展而变得陈旧过时，但礼乐外在的形式或框架却可因补充新的内容而不断获得新的生命。礼的实质是秩序的维持，乐的实质是情感的宣泄。在中国礼乐文化影响下的东方各民族，既重秩序又重情感，而且力求将两者完美地结合起来。在礼乐文化孕育下发展起来的东方文明必将在新的时代新的条件下大放光彩。

中国古代十分重视礼教，教人讲礼敬，懂礼貌，从而形成以恭敬、和顺、谦让等为中心的良好的行为准则和道德规范，千百年来一直流传至今，成为我们的宝贵精神财富。由于礼制、礼仪、礼貌的长期发展和积累，自然会形成一定的礼俗。在漫长的历史岁月中，礼俗是不断变迁的。有的礼俗，富含人文精神，值得继承发扬。但有的礼俗，由于受社会炫富、敛财或低俗等不良风气影响，成了陋俗，则是需要革除的。

本书从《礼记》中精选出 89 则，并加翻译和评析。原文据唐代孔颖达《礼记正义》（清代阮元校刻《十三经注疏》影印本，中华书局1980 年版）。选文和释析，重点不在介绍古代的礼制和礼仪，而在彰显古代的"礼"所富含的人文精神。

Preface

There are thirteen Chinese books composed in ancient times which have been circulating for over two thousand years. These classics are regarded as the origins of Chinese culture. The *Book of Rituals* is one of them.

In the early years of the Western Zhou Dynasty (1046-771 B.C.), Duke Zhou instituted the rituals and music. A book was compiled at that time, and was entitled *Rituals*. It was all about the detailed record of the ceremonial rules.

In the late years of Spring and Autumn period (770-476 B.C.), Confucius established a private school, and books such as *Book of Poetry*, *Book of History*, *Book of Changes*, *Ceremonial Etiquette*, *Book of Music*, *Spring and Autumn*, etc., were chosen as textbooks for students. From the Warring State period (475-221 B.C.) to the early years of the Western Han Dynasty, Confucian scholars wrote articles to illustrate the meanings

of the texts in the *Ceremonial Etiquette*. These articles were very important supplementary materials for teachers who imparted knowledge on rituals. Dai Sheng during the Western Han Dynasty (206 B.C.-25) collected
all these articles into a book entitled *Book of Rituals*.

There are 49 parts in the whole book: 21 parts are about ceremonial
rules, such as "The Meaning of Capping Rituals," "The Meaning of Marriage," etc., 13 parts are on ancient rituals, such as "Royal Regulations,"
"Yue Ling," etc., 8 parts focus on questions and answers between Confucius and his disciples, such as "Zhongni stays idle at home," "Confucius
stays idle at home," "Tan Gong," etc., 7 parts are academic passages,
such as "Ceremonial Usages," "Education on the *Six Classics*," "Record
of Music," "Higher Education," "Central Harmony," "Record on Education," etc.

Book of Rituals is very rich in content. For instance, there are
thoughts and views on politics, society, life, ethics, education, arts, etc.
All these thoughts and views concentrate on the "rituals."

For people who live in modern society, what is the significance and
value of those rituals?

The definition of "ritual" in ancient China is broader than that of
today: 1) it refers to a ritual institution, a hierarchical and ethical order;
2) it refers to the specific ceremonial etiquette; 3) it refers to the social
customs related to rituals; 4) it refers to courtesy, the polite behavior that
shows respect for other people. The first definition is the most important
for it is the core of the rituals.

After the stage of savagery and along with the development of pro-
ductive forces, private ownership and monogamy appeared. When a

state was established, a hierarchical institution and ethical order had to be formed for all members in society. Therefore, human beings began to live in a civilized age.

Rituals were the results of social development. They were born with the private ownership and civilization. Rituals marked the beginning of a civilized society. They will further develop along with social advancement. A higher level of rituals will grow out of a more civilized society and serve to regularize human beings' conducts.

Rituals in the past were all instituted during a specific historical period, thus, they were uniquely expressions of the features of the times. Rituals of a certain dynasty are integral parts of the history of human civilization. Compared with their predecessors, new ideas, thoughts, and opinions may be added to the ritual systems in a later dynasty. The historically accumulative core values share a common nature that belongs to human beings and which transcends the time and space.

For the ancient rituals, we should not affirm everything completely and cling to the outmoded values; neither should we discard all traditions and customs. An appropriate attitude is that we must act in a realistic manner, abandon what is outdated and inherit what is worthy. We must also carry on forward the rituals with an open mind.

The specific ceremonial etiquette is closely related to ritual institutions. In social life, etiquette is no more than just an external form, but it embodies rich content, i.e. the ritual institution and hierarchical order.

According to *Rituals of the Zhou Dynasty*, there were various categories of ceremonial rules: sacrifice rituals (heaven and earth, ancestor, mountains and rivers), funeral rituals (burial, mourning), official rituals (paying respects, mutual visits, forming alliances), military rules (battle, hunting), and auspicious rituals (marriage, feast, arching). Rituals at different levels (capital city, palace, chariot, banners, clothes, containers, seats, music, greetings, etc.) and for different people are associated with strict requirements. The rituals and music instituted by Duke Zhou enabled ancient China to become a state of ceremony and decorum.

Five hundred years after Duke Zhou's period, Confucius established the Confucian School. He inherited the rituals from the past, and also incorporated the idea of "humanity" into the rituals. He emphasized that rituals should not merely be the external institution and order, but also an internal conscience as well. He required that people must restrain their evil desires. Words and deeds should also be in accordance with rituals. Maintaining central harmony is of great significance. People should treat each other kindly and share both duties and obligations. The ancient rituals refer specifically to benevolence in the ruler and loyalty in the subjects, kindness in the father, filial piety in the son, gentility in the elder brother, humility and respect in the younger brother, good behavior in the husband, obedience in the wife, respect for the aged and love for the yang, etc. Confucius thought that some complicated ceremonial rules should have been simplified, for a sincere attitude was more important than the form of practice. Through his efforts, Confucius injected a spirit of humanity into the ritual institutions and rules, which helped elevate Chinese civilization to a higher level.

Confucius also thought that the rituals and music instituted by Duke Zhou were mutually complementary. The views of later Confucian scholars could best demonstrate the concept of central harmony. The institutionalized "rituals" and the spiritual "harmony" bring out the best in each other. A good balance must be kept between the internal peace and the external order. Only when both "rituals" and "harmony" are acquired could a person or a society reach the ideal state.

The specific content of the rituals and music may become outdated along with time, but their external forms could obtain new lives again because of the newly supplemented materials. Maintain a good order is essentially what rituals are for; the fundamental function of music is for emotional release. Oriental people under the influence of Chinese rituals and music treasure both orders and emotions. The oriental civilization grown out of Chinese rituals and music will display more of its brilliance to the world in the new era.

Ancient Chinese people attached great importance to the education on rituals. Showing respect for other people was highly promoted. Being courteous and amicable was required by the code of conducts and moral standards. The core values of rituals have been passed down from generation to generation, and become the precious spiritual wealth. Over the long history of its development, there must be some customs formed, and the customs will also change along with time. Some customs need to be further promoted, for they are expressive of a spirit of humanity; others must be abandoned, because they become vulgar and wasteful.

All 89 entries in this book are selected from *Book of Rituals*. The original Chinese version was edited by a Tang scholar Kong Yingda (574-648) (Beijing: Zhonghua Book Company, 1980). The texts and commentaries we present are not merely to introduce rituals in ancient China, but to demonstrate a spirit of humanity in the rituals as well.

目 录

Contents

目 录
礼记选译

目　录
礼记选译

1. 敖不可长

【原文】

敖不可长，欲不可从，志不可满，乐不可极。

《礼记·曲礼上》

【释文】

傲气不可以滋长，欲望不可以放纵，情志不可以自满，享乐不可以无度。

【解析】

待人接物当谦恭有礼，不可以盛气凌人；生活起居当节俭自律，不可以穷奢极侈。

1.Never allow pride to grow

Never allow pride to grow; never indulge desires; never bring the will to the full; never carry pleasure to excess.

Book of Rituals · Specific Ceremonial Rituals Part 1

【 Commentary 】

A gentleman is respectful, and lives an abstemious way of life. A domineering attitude or an extravagant lifestyle is not recommended.

2. 贤者狎而敬之

【原文】

　　贤者狎而敬之，畏而爱之。爱而知其恶，憎而知其善。积而能散，安安而能迁。临财毋苟得，临难毋苟免。很毋求胜，分毋求多。

　　　　　　　　　　　　　　　　　　《礼记·曲礼上》

【释文】

　　对于贤能的人要亲近并尊敬他，敬畏并爱戴他。对于自己所喜爱的人也要了解他的短处，对于自己所憎恶的人也要了解他的长处。能够积聚财富也能够布施穷人，能够安处当下也能够适时变迁。面对财物不可苟且攫取，面对危难不可苟且逃避。与人争讼不可定求必胜，与人分财不可定求必多。

2.The talented and virtuous men can keep a close relationship with other people, but respect them

The talented and virtuous men can keep a close relationship with other people, but respect them; can stand in awe of other people, but love them. They love other people but acknowledge what evil is in them. They hate other people but recognize what good is in them. Accumulate wealth and also disperse them to help the needy. Be accustomed to circumstances and also willing to move elsewhere. Find wealth within reach, and do not try to acquire it by improper means; meet with calamity, and do not try to escape from it by improper means. Do not seek for victory in disputes; do not seek for more than your proper share.

Book of Rituals · Specific Ceremonial Rituals Part 1

【解析】

　　"礼"的主要精神在"节制"。生活中的"礼"最重"克己"，克制自己，切忌"感情用事"，"好走极端"。比如对自己崇敬的人，也要看到他的缺点和不足；对自己厌恶的人，也要看到他的优点和长处。富贵之时不骄纵，不盛气凌人；贫贱之时不丧志，不屈己从人。财利面前要"见利思义"，不可贪取不义之财；困难面前要"从容应对"，不可丧失志节操守。总之，要中道而行，不偏不倚，无"过"也无"不及"。古人说："礼"的作用，以保持中道与和谐为可贵。

【 Commentary 】

While studying rituals, it is important to know the significance of "limitation." One needs to be able to control oneself and avoid abandoning oneself over to the emotion or going to extremes. For those who respect and admire you, you should not neglect their shortcomings. For those who detest you, you also need to find out their advantages. Do not be too conceited or domineering when you are rich. Do not be too disheartened or subservient when you are poor. Keep honor and duty in mind, and do not take the wealth that is acquired by illegal means. Keep calm when you face difficulties, and always maintain the integrity and moral standards. In a word, one needs to maintain the central way and act impartially, for going too far is as bad as not going far enough. The ancient Chinese believed that rituals would serve to maintain the central way and harmony.

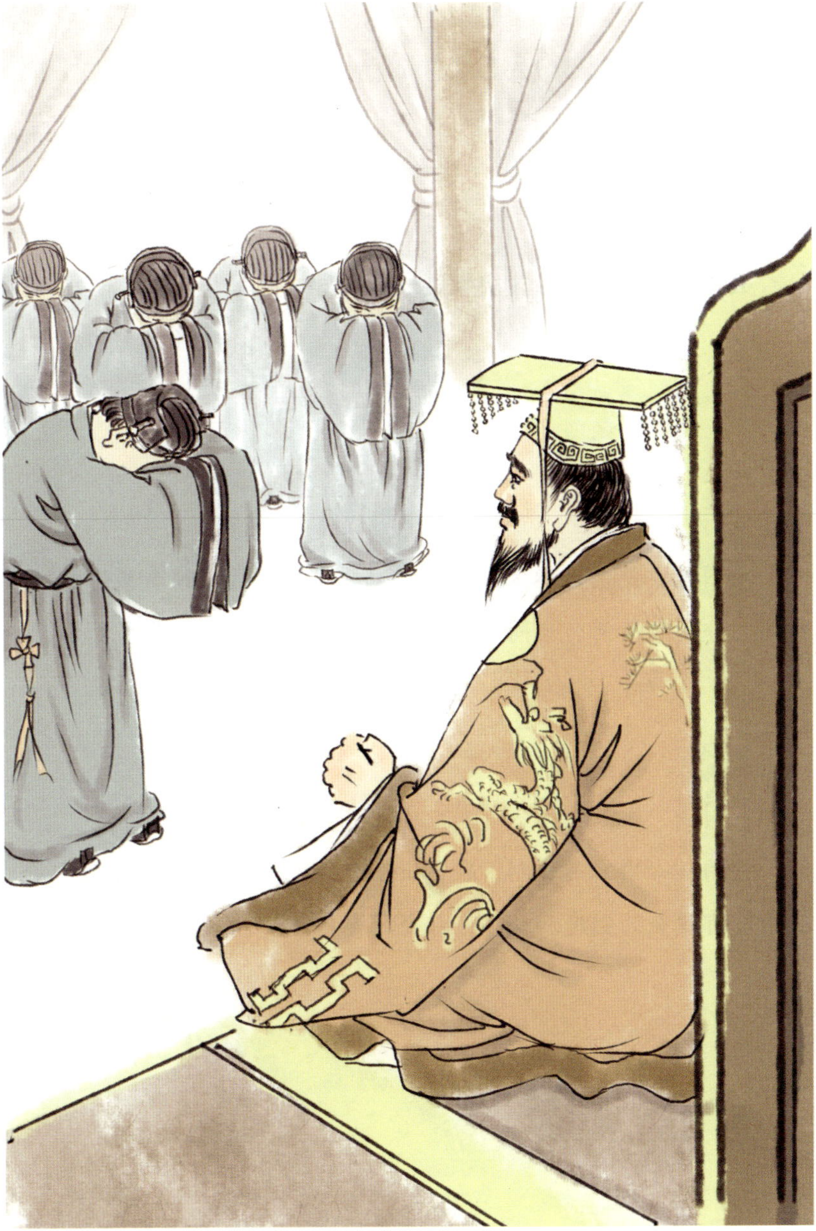

3. 夫礼者所以定亲疏

【原文】

夫礼者所以定亲疏，决嫌疑，别同异，明是非也。

《礼记·曲礼上》

【释文】

所谓礼，是用来确定人与人之间关系的远近，判断事情的疑似难明，分别事情何时当同何时当异，明辨事情有理或无理。

【解析】

礼的核心内容是礼制，是全社会的制度和秩序。一个文明社会，如果没有健全的制度和秩序，社会就会崩溃。

3.The rituals are to determine the observances towards those as close and distant

The rituals are to determine the observances towards those as close and distant; to settle points that may cause suspicion or doubt; to distinguish the differences and similarities; to help tell right from wrong.

Book of Rituals · Specific Ceremonial Rituals Part 1

【 Commentary 】

The core content of the rituals is the system of ceremonial usages, and it is highly relevant to the institution and order of the whole society. A civilized society is featured by a sound system and a proper order. Or else, a societal collapse is just a matter of time.

4. 礼尚往来

【原文】

　　礼尚往来。往而不来，非礼也；来而不往，亦非礼也。人有礼则安，无礼则危。

　　　　　　　　　　　　　　　　　　　　《礼记·曲礼上》

【释文】

　　礼崇尚有往有来。我前往施惠而受惠者不来报答，不合于礼；有人来对我施惠而我不前往报答，也不合于礼。人人有礼社会就会安定，人人无礼社会就会危乱。

【解析】

　　礼崇尚有往有来，是为了构建和谐的人际关系。在社会生活中，人与人，不论贫贱、富贵、长幼、尊卑，都应当互相关心，互相尊重，互相帮助，互相礼让。人人讲礼，人人怀有敬爱和感恩之心，社会才能保持和谐安定。

4.Rituals value reciprocity

Rituals value reciprocity. If I give a gift and receive nothing in return, it is contrary to rituals; if I receive a gift and give nothing in return, it is contrary to rituals as well. If a man acts in accordance with rituals, he is in a condition of security; if he does not do so, he is in danger.

Book of Rituals · Specific Ceremonial Rituals Part 1

【 Commentary 】

Courtesy requires a return of visits received, for this will help build up a harmonious interpersonal relationship. In social life, people should care, respect, help, and show courtesy to each other, no matter you are rich or poor, young or old. When everyone is respectful and courteous, we will see a more stable and harmonious society.

5. 博闻强识而让

博闻强识而让，敦善行而不怠，谓之君子。

《礼记·曲礼上》

【释文】

见闻广博记忆力好而又能谦恭礼让，乐于行善助人而又能长久不懈，这样的人就叫作君子。

【解析】

作为君子，更要谦恭礼让。学问虽好，但不骄纵傲慢；地位虽高，但行善助人不倦。

5.To acquire extensive knowledge and remember retentively, at the same time, he is modest

To acquire extensive knowledge and remember retentively, at the same time, he is modest; to do earnestly what is good, and not become weary in doing so – these are the characteristics of who we call the gentleman.

Book of Rituals · Specific Ceremonial Rituals Part 1

【 Commentary 】

A gentleman is respectful, and courteous. He is knowledgeable, but is never conceited. He is in high position, but is always ready to help others.

6. 礼不下庶人，刑不上大夫

【原文】

礼不下庶人，刑不上大夫。

《礼记·曲礼上》

【释文】

礼制不是为庶人而制，刑罚也不是为卿大夫而设。

【解析】

周公制作礼仪制度，首先要求贵族严格遵守。而一般平民百姓，由于财力不足，在礼仪制度方面，依时变通量力而行即可。至于刑罚，重在惩治或防止奸邪。而卿大夫作为国家重臣，应当自重，严谨守法，不要轻易触犯刑律。如果行为奸邪，就不配继续做卿大夫。

6.The ceremonial rules are not for the common people, and the punishments are not for the great officers

The ceremonial rules are not for the common people, and the punishments are not for the great officers.

Book of Rituals · Specific Ceremonial Rituals Part 1

【 Commentary 】

The noble people must strictly follow the ritual rules formulated by Duke Zhou. As for the commoners, they could carry out the ritual practice as much as their financial resources allow. The punishments were to prevent misdeeds. The great officers should be more cautious and self-disciplined. They must not break the laws. He who commits a misdeed will not be as qualified as a great officer.

7. 称其财，斯之谓礼

【原文】

子路曰："伤哉贫也！生无以为养，死无以为礼也。"孔子曰："啜菽，饮水，尽其欢，斯之谓孝；敛手、足、形，还葬而无椁，称其财，斯之谓礼。"

《礼记·檀弓下》

【释文】

子路说："贫穷真令人忧伤啊！父母在世时没有财力好好供养，父母去世后也没有财力按礼制好好办丧事。"孔子说："父母在世时，尽管是吃豆类，喝凉水，但只要让父母精神愉快，就可以说是孝了。父母死后，尽管尸衣仅够包裹尸体，而且是敛罢立即安葬，有棺而无椁，但只要是同自己的财力相称，也就可以说是合平丧礼的要求了。"

【解析】

周公制作礼仪制度，在丧礼方面有许多具体繁琐的规定。但孔子认为，举办丧事应当量力而行，要同自己的财力相称。孔子还主张丧事从简，认为只要真心表达自己对丧者的哀悼就可以了。

7.Perform as much as his means allow, he can be said to discharge sufficiently the rituals

Zilu said, "Alas for the poor! When their parents are alive, they do not have the means to support them; and when their parents are dead, they do not have the means to perform the mourning and burial rituals for them." Confucius said, "Eat bean food and drink cold water. As long as their parents are made happy, this is nothing less than filial piety. If a son can only wrap the body of his deceased parents round from head to foot, and inter his parents immediately albeit without a shell, and carry this out as much as his means allow, he can be said to discharge sufficiently the rituals of mourning and burial."

Book of Rituals · Tan Gong Part 2

【 Commentary 】

Duke Zhou formulated the ceremonial rituals at that time and there were a large number of specific rules on the funeral rituals. According to Confucius, funeral ceremonies should be carried out as much as the resources allow. And he advocated a simple practice of funeral rituals, and asserted that it would be sufficient as long as the condolences were sincerely expressed.

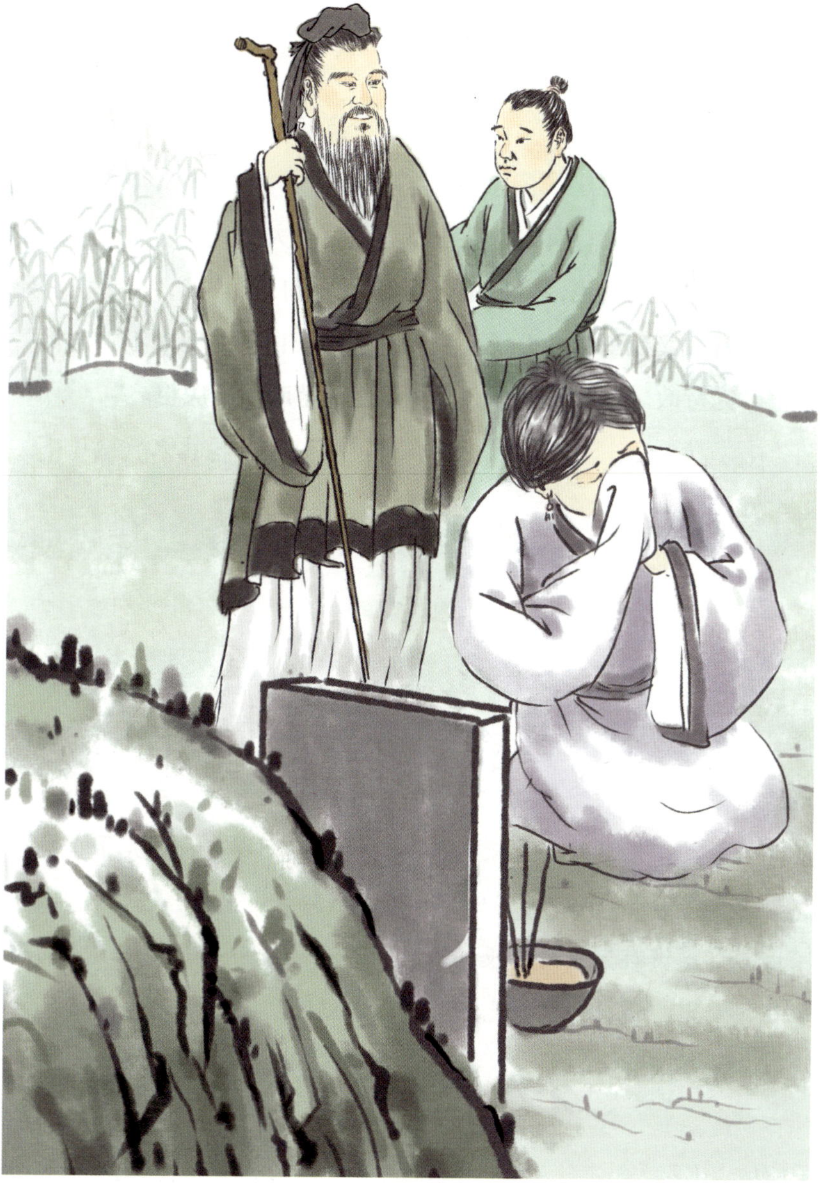

8. 苛政猛于虎

【原文】

孔子过泰山侧，有妇人哭于墓者而哀。夫子式而听之，使子贡问之曰："子之哭也，壹似重有忧者。"而曰："然，昔者吾舅死于虎，吾夫又死焉，今吾子又死焉。"夫子曰："何为不去也？"曰："无苛政。"夫子曰："小子识之，苛政猛于虎也。"

《礼记·檀弓下》

【释文】

孔子从泰山旁路过，看见一个妇人在墓前哭得很悲伤。孔子就停车凭轼听她哭，然后让子贡去问那位妇人："听您的哭声，好像遭遇不幸有深重的忧伤。"妇人回答道："是的。过去我的公公被老虎咬死了，接着我的丈夫又被老虎咬死了，现在我的儿子也被老虎咬死了。"孔子问道："那您为什么不离开这里呢？"妇人答道："因为这里没有繁重的徭役和赋税。"孔子对弟子们说："你们要记住，繁重的徭役和赋税比老虎还要凶猛啊！"

8.Oppressive government is more ferocious than tigers

Confucius passed by the side of Mountain Tai, and encountered a woman who was wailing bitterly by a grave. The Master bowed forward to the chariot cross-bar and listened to her. Then he sent Zigong to question her. "Your wailing," said he, "is altogether like that of a person who has suffered from great sorrow." She replied, "It is so. My father-in-law was killed by a tiger. My husband was also killed by another tiger. Now my son has been killed in the same way." The Master said, "Why not leave the place?" The answer was, "There is no oppressive government here." The Master then said to the disciples, "Remember this, my disciples. Oppressive government is more ferocious than tigers."

Book of Rituals · Tan Gong Part 2

【解析】

　　繁苛的政令主要指繁重的徭役和赋税。春秋末年，各诸侯国的统治者，为了满足自己无尽的贪欲，往往强迫民众频繁地服劳役、兵役，无休止地增加民众的赋税，使民不聊生，民众大批死亡。孔子以仁爱之心，对遭受苦难的民众深表同情，怒斥统治者的繁苛政令比老虎还要凶猛。

【 Commentary 】

An oppressive government will bring heavy corvee and tax to its people. In the late years of the Spring and Autumn period, rulers in various vassal states, in order to satiate their greedy desires, often forced their people to do hard labor or serve in the army. In addition, they ceaselessly raised the taxes on the commoners who lived on the edge of starvation. All these resulted in the death of a great number of people. Confucius expressed his sympathy on those who suffered from hardships and misfortunes. He indignantly criticized an oppressive government which was even more ferocious than real tigers.

9. 天民之穷而无告者也，皆有常饩

少而无父者谓之孤，老而无子者谓之独，老而无妻者谓之矜，老而无夫者谓之寡。此四者，天民之穷而无告者也，皆有常饩。瘖、聋、跛、躃、断者、侏儒，百工各以其器食之。

《礼记·王制》

【释文】

年幼而失去父亲的人叫作孤，年老而失去或没有儿子的人叫作独，年老而失去妻子的人叫作矜，年老而失去丈夫的人叫作寡。这四种人，是上天降生的民众中最困难而又求告无门的人，国家对他们要经常性地发给粮食给予救济。哑巴、聋子、跛子、瘸子、肢体残缺者、躯体矮小者，让他们凭各自的手艺干点力所能及的工作，而由国家养活他们。

【解析】

每个时代，社会上都会有矜寡孤独和肢体残缺的人，他们往往不能自食其力而需要获得救助。因此，国家要关心他们，要用各种方式从物质上救济他们，让他们的物质生活得到保障。

9.The most forlorn people who had none to whom to tell their wants received regular allowances

One who lost his father at a young age was called an orphan. An old man who lost his sons was called a solitary. An old man who lost his wife was called a widower. An old woman who lost her husband was called a widow. These four classes were the most forlorn of heaven's people, and had no one to tell their wants; they all received regular allowances. The dumb, the deaf, and the lame, the pigmies, were all fed according to what work they were able to do.

Book of Rituals · Royal Regulation

【 Commentary 】

In every age, there are orphans, solitaries, widows, widowers and the disabled people. They probably are not able to earn their own living and need support. Therefore, they should be taken care of by the country and provided with financial support.

10. 大同

【原文】

孔子曰："大道之行也，天下为公。选贤与能，讲信修睦，故人不独亲其亲，不独子其子，使老有所终，壮有所用，幼有所长，矜寡孤独废疾者，皆有所养。男有分，女有归。货恶其弃于地也，不必藏于己；力恶其不出于身也，不必为己。是故谋闭而不兴，盗窃乱贼而不作，故外户而不闭。是谓大同。"

《礼记·礼运》

【释文】

孔子说："大道实行的时代，天下是公有的，大家推选有道德有才能的人为领袖，人与人之间十分讲求诚信，不断增进和睦。所以人们不只是亲爱和孝敬自己的双亲，不只是慈爱和抚养自己的子女，使老年人都能得到终养，壮年人都有能用其力的地方，幼年人都能健康成长，矜寡孤独和残疾的人，都能得到社会的照顾和赡养。男子都有自己的一份职业，女子都能适时出嫁成家。对于财物，人们只是厌恶它被糟踏浪费因而去努力生产或保有，但努力生产不一定都归自己所有；对于气力，人们只是厌恶它不尽量地从自己身上发出来，但努力劳动不一定是为了自己。因此阴谋诡计被扼制封杀而不能兴风作浪，盗贼偷盗和乱臣贼子的叛逆也不会发生，因此外面的门户晚上不用上锁。这就叫大同社会。"

10.The Great Commonwealth

When the great Way prevailed, the world was a common state. Rulers were selected according to their wisdom and ability. Mutual confidence and peace prevailed. Therefore, people not only regarded their own parents as parents and their own children as children. The old were able to enjoy their old age, the young were able to employ their talent, the juniors had the elders to look up to, and the helpless widows, orphans and cripples and disabled were well taken care of. The men had their respective occupations and the women had their homes. If the people did not want to see goods lying about on the ground, they did not have to keep them for themselves, and if people had too much energy for work, they did not have to labor for their own profit. Therefore, there was no cunning or intrigue and there were no bandits or burglars, and as a result, there was no need to shut one's outer gate at night. This was the period of Datong, or the Great Commonwealth.

Book of Rituals · Ceremonial Usages

【解析】

孔子所描绘的大同社会，生产资料和生活资料都是公有的，生产和分配都体现了"我为人人，人人为我"。大家选举贤能的人为领袖，来管理大家的事。在这样的社会里，人尽所能，物尽其用。老年人，未成年人，矜寡孤独和残疾的人，都能得到社会的照顾和赡养。人与人之间讲求诚信，和睦相处。社会安定和平，人人安居乐业。孔子所赞赏的大同社会，与其说是对上古时代的追忆，不如说是对未来社会的憧憬。在今天，孔子的大同理想，仍能鼓舞和激励我们前进，甚至提供了宝贵的借鉴，指导我们去建设美好的家园。

【 Commentary 】

The Datong society, or the Great Commonwealth, that described by Confucius was a common state. All resources were publicly owned. The production and distribution of goods were fairly carried out for each and every member of the society. The worthy people were chosen as the rulers. Everyone could give full play to his or her talents and everything could be served their proper purposes. The old and young, the widows and widowers, the orphans and the disabled were all supported by the whole society. People were sincere and trustful. A harmonious atmosphere prevailed in a stable and peaceful society. Everyone worked and lived in peace. The Datong society that Confucius admired was not only what he treasured in the past, but also what he expected in the future. The Datong ideal provides us with an exemplar case and still serves as the driving force to build a better world.

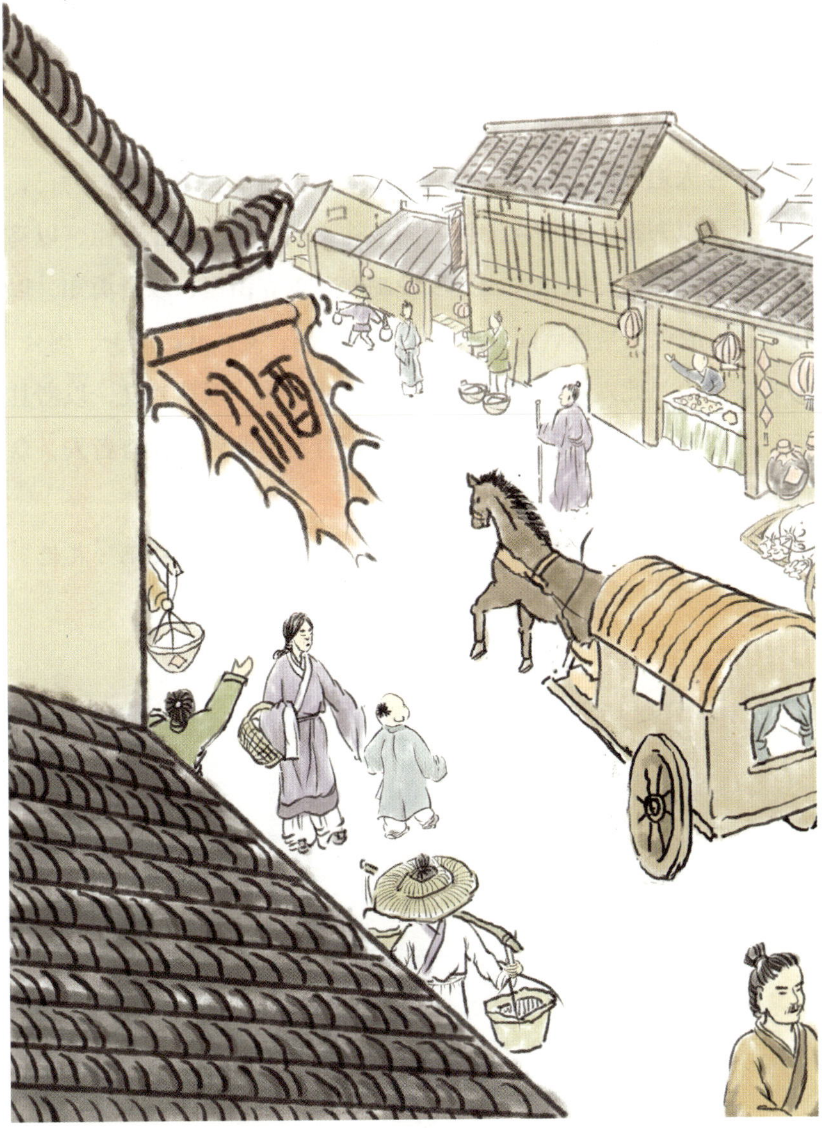
酒

11. 小康

"今大道既隐，天下为家，各亲其亲，各子其子，货力为己，大人世及以为礼，城郭沟池以为固，礼义以为纪，以正君臣，以笃父子，以睦兄弟，以和夫妇，以设制度，以立田里，以贤勇知，以功为己，故谋用是作，而兵由此起。禹、汤、文、武、成王、周公，由此其选也。此六君子者，未有不谨于礼者也。以著其义，以考其信，著有过，刑仁讲让，示民有常。如有不由此者，在势者去，众以为殃。是谓小康。"

《礼记·礼运》

【释文】

"如今大同社会天下为公的大道已经隐没不行了，天下成为君王一家的天下，人们各自亲爱自己的双亲，各自亲爱自己的子女，财货都尽力据为己有，把王公贵族世代相袭作为礼，修筑内城外城和护城河来加固防守，把礼义作为纲纪和原则，用来规范君臣关系，用来加深父子感情，用来使兄弟和睦，用来使夫妇和美，用来建立制度，用来划分田地和居里，用来表彰有勇有智的人，用来为自己

11.The Minor Peace

But now the great Way no longer prevails, and the world is divided up into private families, and people regard only their own parents as parents and only their own children as children. They acquire goods and labor each for their own benefit. A hereditary aristocracy is established and the different states build cities, outer cities and moat each for its own defense. The principles of rituals, or forms of social intercourse and honor and duty, serve as the principles of social discipline. By means of these principles, people try to maintain the official status of rulers and subjects, to teach the parents and children, elder and younger brothers, husbands and wives, to live in harmony, to establish social institutions and to live in groups of hamlets. The physically strong and the mentally clever are raised to prominence, and each one tries to carve his own career. Hence there is deceit and cunning and from these wars arise. The great founders of dynasties life, the Emperors Yu, Tang, Wen, Wu and Cheng and Duke Zhou were the best men of this age. Without a single exception, these six gentlemen were deeply concerned over the principles of rituals, through which justice was maintained, general confidence was tested, and errors or malpractices were exposed. And ideal of humanity was set up and good manners were cultivated, as solid principles for the common people to follow. A ruler who violates these principles would then be denounced as a public enemy and driven off from

建立功业。这样一来阴谋算计的事就随之而生，兵戎相见的事也因此而起。夏禹、商汤、周文王、武王、成王、周公，就是在这种情况下产生的以礼义治天下的英杰。这六位君子，没有一个不是恭谨实行礼制的。他们用礼来彰显道义，考察诚信，指明过失，推崇仁爱，讲究礼让，向百姓显示一切都有常规必须遵循。如不遵循礼义，在上位的权势者要被废黜，民众都把他看作祸殃。这就叫作小康。"

【解析】

　　这一则承上，仍然是孔子说的话。孔子认为，继远古大同社会之后出现的是小康社会，具体来说，指夏、商、周三代。这时天下私有代替了天下公有，因而普遍出现了阴谋算计和武力争斗。但三代创业之君，恭谨实行礼制，遵礼法，讲道义，崇仁爱，重伦理，因此社会秩序井然有序，民众安居乐业。孔子又认为，他所生活的春秋末年为乱世，应加以改造。改造的途径分两步，第一步实行礼制，建成夏、商、周三代开创时那样的小康社会，第二步实行天下公有，建成大同社会。

his office. This is called the Period of Xiaokang, or Minor Peace.

Book of Rituals · Ceremonial Usages

【 Commentary 】

This entry continued from the previous one, both of which were words of Confucius. According to him, the period that followed Datong was Xiaokang, and it specifically referred to the Xia, Shang and Zhou Dynasties. The whole world was divided into private families, but not a common state. Evil schemes and violent fights were taking their rise. But the founding fathers of those three dynasties acted strictly in accordance with rituals. They respected laws, valued duty and honor, and laid stress on moral standards. Therefore, the societies in general were in good order and the people could live and work in peace. Confucius also thought that actions were needed to improve the riotous society that he lived in during the late years of the Spring and Autumn period. Firstly, a sound ritual system should be established so as to build a Xiaokang society that may echo the prosperous periods in the early years of those three dynasties. Secondly, the world should be built into a common state, so that the Great Commonwealth can be achieved.

12. 治人七情，修十义

【原文】

　　"何谓人情？喜、怒、哀、惧、爱、恶、欲七者，弗学而能。何谓人义？父慈、子孝、兄良、弟弟、夫义、妇听、长惠、幼顺、君仁、臣忠十者，谓之人义。讲信修睦，谓之人利。争夺相杀，谓之人患。故圣人之所以治人七情，修十义，讲信修睦，尚辞让，去争夺，舍礼何以治之？"

《礼记·礼运》

【释文】

　　"什么叫作人的感情？欢喜、愤怒、悲哀、恐惧、热爱、厌恶、欲求，这七种不学就会的感情就叫作人的感情。什么叫作做人的道理？父母慈爱，子女孝敬，兄长友爱，幼弟恭顺，丈夫讲义，妻子听从，长者惠下，幼者顺上，君主仁慈，臣下忠诚，这十种维系人际关系的准则就叫作做人的道理。讲求信用，增进和睦，这就是人的利益所在。互相争夺，互相残杀，这就是人的祸患所在。圣人要想疏导人的七情，培育这十种维系人际关系的做人的道理，弘扬谦让美德，避免争夺之害，除了礼以外，就没有其他更好的办法。"

12.Cultivate the seven emotions and the ten duties

What is human nature? It consists of the seven emotions, joy, anger, sorrow, fear, love, hatred and desire, all of which do not have to be learned. What are human duties? Kindness in the father, filial piety in the son, gentility in the elder brother, humility and respect in the younger brother, good behavior in the husband, obedience in the wife, benevolence in the elders, and obedience in the juniors, benevolence in the ruler and loyalty in the subjects—these ten are the human duties. What is good for mankind means general confidence and peace, and what is bad for mankind means struggle for profit, robbery and murder. Therefore, to cultivate the seven emotions and the ten duties, and to promote mutual confidence and peace and courtesy and discourage the struggle for profit and robbery, if the sage, or ideal ruler, dispense with rituals in his efforts, how will he succeed?

Book of Rituals · Ceremonial Usages

【解析】

孔子认为，每个人都有情欲，这是自然的本能，是天生的，合理的，正当的。但孔子又认为，每个人的情欲，必须用礼义来节制，来引导，人与人之间，应当用伦理道德来约束。孔子提出的父母慈爱、子女孝敬、兄长友爱、幼弟恭顺、丈夫讲义、妻子听从、长者惠下、幼者顺上、君主仁慈、臣下忠诚这十种维系人际关系的准则，就是最重要的伦理道德，是我们做人的根本道理。

【 Commentary 】

According to Confucius, every one of us has desires which are inborn and reasonable. He also thought that rituals must be employed to restrain the excess of desires and moral standards must be used to discipline interpersonal relationship. The ten duties that Confucius put forward, namely, kindness in the father, filial piety in the son, gentility in the elder brother, humility and respect in the younger brother, good behavior in the husband, obedience in the wife, benevolence in the elders, and obedience in the juniors, benevolence in the ruler and loyalty in the subjects, are the most important moral standards and fundamental principles for human conduct.

13. 礼义也者，人之大端也

【原文】

"故礼义也者，人之大端也，所以讲信修睦而固人之肌肤之会、筋骸之束也，所以养生送死事鬼神之大端也，所以达天道顺人情之大窦也。故唯圣人为知礼之不可以已也。故坏国、丧家、亡人，必先去其礼。"

《礼记·礼运》

【释文】

"所以说，礼义这个东西是做人最基本的准则。人们用礼来讲求信用，增进和睦，从而使彼此亲密得就像肌肤相接、筋骨相连一样。人们把礼作为养生送死和敬事鬼神最基本的准则，把礼作为贯彻天理、理顺人情最重要的渠道。所以只有圣人才知道礼是须臾不可废弃的，因此，凡是国亡家破身败的人，一定是由于他先废弃了礼。"

【解析】

孔子认为，礼义是做人最基本的准则。对处在上位的人来说，坚守礼义，就会增进和睦，国家兴旺；废弃礼义，就会国亡家破，自取灭亡。

13. Rituals and duties are the main principles of human life

Therefore, rituals and duties are the main principles of human life, serving the purpose of promoting mutual confidence and social harmony and strengthening the social ties and bonds of friendship. They are the main principles for worshipping the spirits and feeding the living and sacrificing to the dead. Ritual is a great channel through which we follow the laws of the heaven and direct to proper course the expressions of the human heart. Therefore, only the sage knows that rituals are indispensable. Therefore, to destroy a kingdom, upset a family or ruin a man, you must first take away from him this sense of rituals.

Book of Rituals · Ceremonial Usages

【 Commentary 】

Confucius asserted that rituals and duties were the most fundamental principles of human life. Men in authority will help promote social harmony and strengthen the social ties, if rituals are maintained. They will bring the ruin of states and the destruction of families, if rituals are abandoned.

14. 礼也者，义之实也

【原文】

礼也者，义之实也。

《礼记·礼运》

【释文】

礼制是道义的实际体现。

【解析】

孔子认为，礼之实质在义。就是说，礼制的根源在道义，礼制是根据道义制定出来的，礼制必须符合道义。

14.Rituals are the embodiment of honor and duty

Rituals are the embodiment of honor and duty.

Book of Rituals · Ceremonial Usages

【 Commentary 】

According to Confucius, rituals represent honor and duty. Rituals take root in honor and duty. Hence, any ceremonial rituals and usages of social life must be formed in accordance with honor and duty.

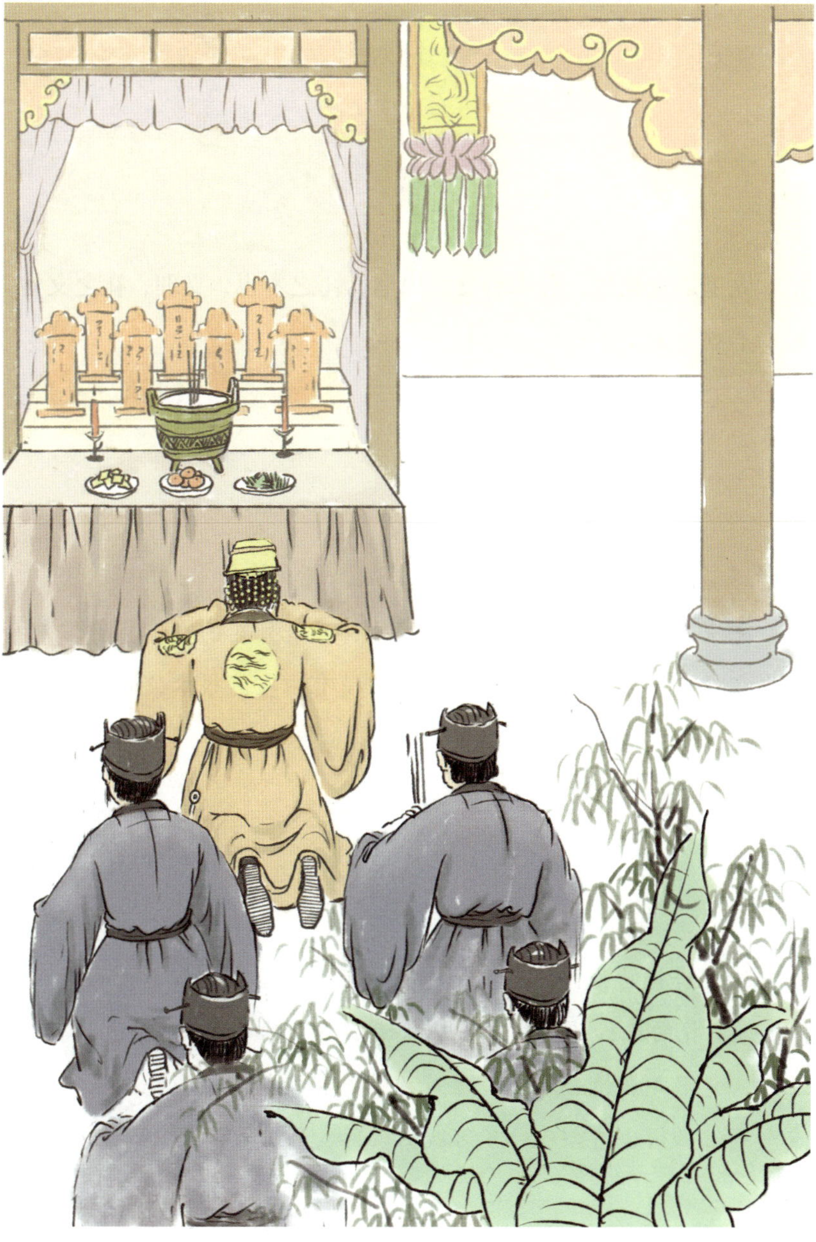

15. 先王之立礼也，有本有文

【原文】

先王之立礼也，有本有文。忠信，礼之本也；义理，礼之文也。无本不立，无文不行。

《礼记·礼器》

【释文】

先王制定的礼，既有内在的根本，又有外在的文饰。忠信是礼的内在根本，义理是礼的外在文饰。没有内在的根本，礼就不能树立；没有外在的文饰，礼就无法施行。

【解析】

这里讲礼的施行。忠信，意思是忠心诚信。忠信是礼的内在根本，说明礼的施行必须建立在忠心诚信的基础之上，不可表里不一。义理，意思是合情合理。义理是礼的外在文饰，说明礼的施行在外在形式上必须合情合理，不可脱离实际，违背人情事理。

15.The rituals formulated by the ancient kings had their internal content and their external form

The rituals formulated by the ancient kings had their internal content and their external form. A true heart and good faith are their internal content. The characteristics of what is fair and reasonable are their external form. Rituals could not have been established without the internal content. Rituals could not have been put into practice without the external form.

Book of Rituals · Rituals in the Formation of Character

【 Commentary 】

This entry emphasizes the practice of rituals. Loyalty and trustfulness are the core values of rituals, upon which the whole ceremonial institution should be established. The external form of rituals requires that the practice must be carried out in a realistic and reasonable manner.

16. 伊耆氏始为蜡

【原文】

伊耆氏始为蜡。……曰："土反其宅，水归其壑，昆虫毋作，草木归其泽。"

《礼记·郊特牲》

【释文】

从伊耆氏开始才有蜡祭。……祭时祝祷道："泥土回到原来的地方，水流回到原来的河床，昆虫不要兴起，草木仍旧生长到沼泽里。"

【解析】

伊耆氏即传说中原始社会的神农氏。他教民稼穑，于是农业便发展起来。农业生产最惧怕水灾、虫灾等灾害，因此每年冬天都要举行祭祀百神的蜡祭。祭祀时祭司往往在祝辞中祈求百神保佑，希望来年不要发生水、旱、虫、草等灾害，以保农作物丰收。从这里，可以看到远古的祭礼与人们现实生活息息相关。

16. The great sacrifice was first instituted by Yiqi

The great sacrifice was first instituted by Yiqi...They said, "Soils go back to the original places; water flows in its channels; insects keep quiet; weeds grow only in fen lands."

Book of Rituals · Border Sacrifices

【 Commentary 】

Yiqi was the legendary Shennong, or Divine Husbandman, in ancient times. It was Shennong who taught the people to grow crops. Farmers hate flood and plague of insects. Each year, there was a great sacrifice. The sacrificial priests would pray for the blessings from various gods and spirits. They hoped that there would be no flood, drought or plague of insects, so that a good harvest could be guaranteed. From this entry, we can tell that the sacrifice ceremony in the past was highly relevant to real life.

17. 天地合而后万物兴

　　天地合而后万物兴焉。夫昏礼，万世之始也。取于异姓，所以附远厚别也。

《礼记·郊特牲》

【释文】

　　天与地相配交合然后万物兴起。男子与女子举行婚礼结为夫妻，也是繁衍子孙以至万代的开始。娶异姓女子为妻，这是为了同血缘关系疏远的人结亲，以严格区分与隔绝同血缘相近的人的婚配。

【解析】

　　古人认为，男女婚配是繁衍后代使人丁兴旺的大事，其意义可与天地繁衍万物相比拟，因而十分重视婚礼，并制订了从请媒求亲、致送聘礼、请示婚期直至男子亲迎的具体程序，称为"六礼"。古人从人类自身漫长的历史中，又认识到近亲结婚会严重影响后代身体发育，因而主张"同姓不婚"。这些都具有积极意义。

17.The union between the heaven and the earth makes all things prosper

The union between the heaven and the earth makes all things prosper. The ceremony of marriage is the beginning of myriad generations. The wife should be with a different surname. Therefore, it is important to bring those who are distant together, and keep those who are of the same surnames separate.

Book of Rituals · Border Sacrifices

【 Commentary 】

According to ancient Chinese, marriage is such a significant issue for a large family that it is no less important than the union of the heaven and the earth. They formulated six specific rules of marriage rituals to regulate the whole process from the engagement to the wedding. They also realized that marriages between people who are close blood relatives would result in healthy problems for the offspring. All these views were of great significance.

18. 柔声以谏

【原文】

父母有过，下气怡色，柔声以谏。谏若不入，起敬起孝，说则复谏；不说，与其得罪于乡党州闾，宁孰谏。父母怒、不说，而挞之流血，不敢疾怨，起敬起孝。

《礼记·内则》

【释文】

父母有了过错，做子女的要低声下气、和颜悦色地劝谏。父母如果不听从劝谏，做子女的就应更加恭敬更加孝顺，等到他们高兴的时候再次劝谏；再次劝谏也可能让父母更不高兴，但是与其让父母由于他们的过错而得罪于邻里乡党，宁可自己犯颜苦谏。如果犯颜苦谏使得父母大怒，把自己打得皮破血流，那也不敢埋怨父母，而是对父母更加恭敬更加孝顺，继续劝谏。

18.A filial son will admonish a parent benignly

If a parent commits a fault, a filial son will admonish a parent benignly. If the parent does not listen to it, the son will be more reverential and more filial. If the parent is happy with this, the son will repeat the admonition. If the parent is unhappy, the son will strongly remonstrate, because it is better than allow the parent to commit an offence against any neighbors. If the parent is angry and even unhappier, and beats him till the blood flows, the son will not be angry and resentful, but still be more reverential and more filial.

Book of Rituals · Family Principles

【解析】

　　古代的孝道，提倡孝顺父母。但这种孝顺，不是无原则的盲从。当父母有了过错时，做子女的要加以劝谏。而这种劝谏，又与劝谏他人不同。子女劝谏父母应当和颜悦色，绝不可大声呵斥。子女孝顺父母，应以服从道义为前提。父母的话符合道义，子女自当顺从；父母的话如果违背道义，子女应当进行劝谏。古人认为，从义不从父，才是真正的大孝。

【 Commentary 】

Filial piety in ancient China was not a virtue that required sons and daughters to maintain in a blind manner. When parents commit faults, sons and daughters should admonish them. Yet it is a different kind of admonishment, for a filial son will never reproach his parents in a loud voice, instead, he will admonish them benignly. Sons and daughters should obey their parents' order if it is in accordance with moral standards; they should admonish their parents, if the order is against the spirit of honor and duty. The real filial piety lies not in the blind obedience of parents, but in adherence to the moral standards.

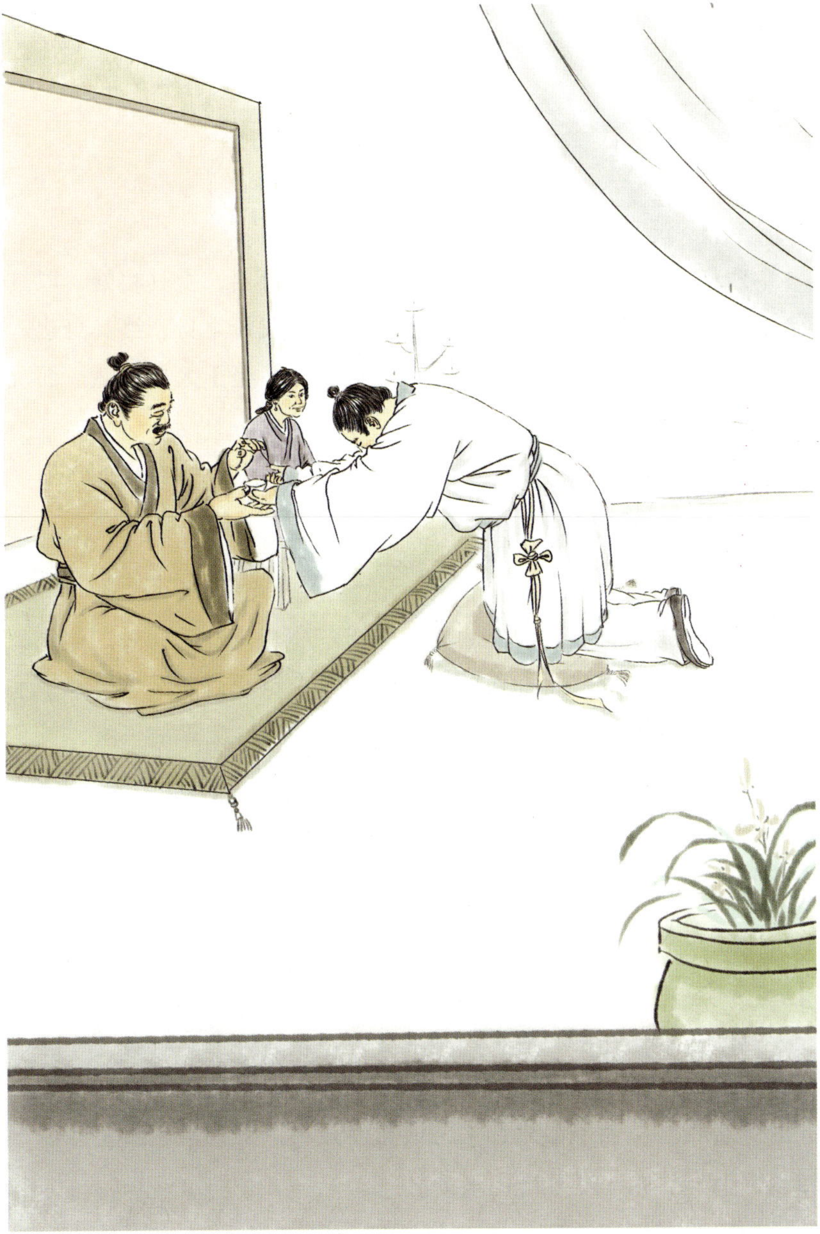

19. 孝子之养老

【原文】

　　孝子之养老也，乐其心不违其志，乐其耳目，安其寝处，以其饮食忠养之，孝子之身终。终身也者，非终父母之身，终其身也。是故父母之所爱亦爱之，父母之所敬亦敬之，至于犬马尽然，而况于人乎！

《礼记·内则》

【释文】

　　孝子的养老，要使父母内心快乐而不违背他们的意愿，要使父母耳目愉悦，起居安适，在饮食方面则尽心照顾周到，直到孝子本人死而后已。所谓"终身"孝敬父母，不是说终父母的一生，而是终孝子自己的一生。因此，尽管父母已经去世，但他们生前所爱的，子女也要爱；他们生前所敬的，子女也要敬；就是对他们喜欢的犬马也都是如此对待，更何况对他们爱敬的人呢！

【解析】

　　这里说的是子女应当怎样孝敬父母：在精神上要顺从父母的心意，使他们感到高兴；在物质生活上要照顾好父母，使他们在饮食、居住、娱乐等方面都能得到悉心照料而感到满足。子女终其一生，都要保持对父母始终不渝的敬爱。

19.A filial son in nourishing his parents

While nourishing his parents, a filial son will make them happy, and never go against their wishes. He will promote their comfort in their bedrooms and supply them with drink and food. A filial son will carry this out to the end of life. "The end of life" does not refer to the end of parents' lives, but the end of the filial son's own life. Hence, he will love what his parents love, and respect what they respect. He will do the same to their dogs and horses, let alone the men they love and respect!

Book of Rituals · Family Principles

【 Commentary 】

This entry shows how to act as a filial son or daughter to parents: a filial son or daughter will always make the parents happy and never go against their wishes; a filial son or daughter will devote all his or her attention to the utmost care of parents, and enable them to a satisfied diet and way of life; a filial son or daughter should unswervingly love and respect the parents to the end of life.

20. 玉不琢，不成器

　　玉不琢，不成器；人不学，不知道。是故古之王者，建国君民，教学为先。

《礼记·学记》

【释文】

　　玉石不经过雕琢，就不能成为器物；人不经过学习，就不会懂得道理。所以古代的君王，建立国家，统治民众，首先要兴办学校，对年轻人施行教育。

【解析】

　　一个人只有经过学习，接受教育，才会懂得道理，成为有用的人才。因此，一个国家，一个社会，必须高度重视兴办学校，培养人才。这里提出了"国家应以教育为本"的重要观点。

20. A piece of jade cannot become an object of art without chiseling

A piece of jade cannot become an object of art without chiseling, and a man cannot come to know the moral law without education. Therefore, the ancient kings regarded the instruction and establishment of schools as the priority in their efforts to build states and rule the people.

Book of Rituals · Record on Education

【 Commentary 】

After receiving a good education, a person acquires more knowledge and can serve the society better. Therefore, men in authority should attach great importance to the establishment of schools and cultivation of professionals. The point that "the fate of a country lies in education" is emphasized in this entry.

21. 教学相长

【原文】

　　虽有嘉肴，弗食，不知其旨也；虽有至道，弗学，不知其善也。是故学然后知不足，教然后知困。知不足，然后能自反也；知困，然后能自强也。故曰教学相长也。

《礼记·学记》

【释文】

　　尽管有非常可口的菜肴，如果不吃就不会知道它的美味；尽管有非常高深的道理，如果不学就不会知道它的精妙。由此可见，只有通过学习才能知道自己的不足，通过教人才能知道自己困惑的地方。知道自己的不足，然后才能反身自省严格要求自己；知道自己困惑的地方，然后才能奋发图强。所以说，教与学是互相促进的。

【解析】

　　教与学是互相促进的，是说一位教师教学生，传道授业，固然是施与，是付出，但在传道授业过程中，必然会感到自己的不足与困惑，从而推动自己不断地学习，不断地增长知识，完善道德，这对自己来说，又是收获，是充实和提高。这是人们在长期教学实践中所获得的认识，揭示出教育工作的一个普遍规律。后来人们把教师与学生的互教共学，也看成是另一种教与学的互相促进。

21.The processes of teaching and learning stimulate one another

One cannot know the taste of food without eating it, however delicious it may be. Therefore, without education one cannot come to know the excellence of knowledge, although it may be there. Therefore, only through education does one come to be dissatisfied with his own knowledge, and only through teaching others does one come to realize the inadequacy of his knowledge. Being dissatisfied with his own knowledge, one then realizes that the trouble lies with himself, and realizing the inadequacy of his knowledge, one then feels stimulated to improve himself. Therefore, it is said, "The processes of teaching and learning stimulate one another."

Book of Rituals · Record on Education

【 Commentary 】

Teaching and learning improve each other. The teacher imparts what he had learned to his students. In the process of teaching, the teacher knows his own deficiencies, and this will stimulate himself to learn more and elevate his moral standards. For the teacher himself, teaching is a rewarding process. The last sentence comes from the teaching practice and it is also a universal rule in education. The interactive processes of teaching and learning are indeed mutually beneficial.

22. 教之所由兴

【原文】

　　大学之法，禁于未发之谓豫，当其可之谓时，不陵节而施之谓孙，相观而善之谓摩。此四者，教之所由兴也。

《礼记·学记》

【释文】

　　大学教育学生的法则是这样的，当问题尚未萌发之时先行约束就叫"预防"，当条件成熟之时及时进行教育就叫"及时"，不超越阶段而有序地施行教育就叫"循序渐进"，互相观察互相学习互相促进就叫"观摩而善"。这四条，就是使教育不断走向成功的方法。

【解析】

　　这里讲的是大学教育学生的几项基本原则：一、教育要有预见，先做预防，防患于未然；二、教育要及时，要在最恰当的时候及时施教；三、教育要循序渐进，不可脱离实际、操之过急；四、教育要注重互相观摩，互相激励。

22.Reasons for the success of education

The principles of higher education are as follows: first, prevention, or preventing bad habits before they arise; secondly, timeliness, or giving the students things when they are ready for them; thirdly, order, or teaching the different subjects in proper sequence; fourthly, mutual stimulation, or letting the students admire the excellence of other students. These four things are the reasons for the success of education.

Book of Rituals · Record on Education

【 Commentary 】

There are four basic rules for the students of higher education to remember and practice: firstly, take preventive measures against anything evil; secondly, apply appropriate methods in a timely manner; thirdly, follow a proper order and avoid acting with undue haste; fourthly, attach great importance to mutual observation and encouragement.

23. 教之所由废

【原文】

发然后禁，则扞格而不胜；时过然后学，则勤苦而难成；杂施而不孙，则坏乱而不修；独学而无友，则孤陋而寡闻；燕朋逆其师；燕辟废其学。此六者，教之所由废也。

《礼记·学记》

【释文】

错误发生了再去禁止，学生就容易产生抵触而难于制止；错过了学习的最佳时机，事后尽管勤苦努力也难于取得成功；杂乱地施教而不循序渐进，失去条理后教学秩序就难以收拾；独自学习而不与朋友讨论切磋，就会使自己学识浅薄见闻不广；与不正派的朋友交往，就会违逆老师的教导；做一些不正经的事，就会荒废当前的学业。这六点，就是教育失败的原因。

【解析】

前四点，紧承上则，再从反面来说，指出教育失败的原因。后面补充的两点，指出求学的人如果交友不当（与不正派的朋友交往），行事不当（做不正经的事），也会使教育失败。

23.The causes for the breakdown of education

To forbid students after they have already acquired bad habits would seem to make everything go against their grain and efforts at correction would be without success. To teach them when the young age is past would make their learning difficult and futile. To fail to teach the different subjects in their proper order would bring about chaos in their studies, without good results. To study a subject all alone without friends would make a student too narrow in scope, lacking in general knowledge. Bad company would encourage them to go against their teachers and bad pastimes would cause them to neglect their studies. These six things cause the breakdown of education.

Book of Rituals · Record on Education

【 Commentary 】

This entry points out the reasons for the breakdown of education. It highlights that bad companies and pastimes will also lead to failure in education.

24. 学者有四失

【原文】

学者有四失，教者必知之。人之学也，或失则多，或失则寡，或失则易，或失则止。此四者，心之莫同也。知其心，然后能救其失也。教也者，长善而救其失者也。

《礼记·学记》

【释文】

求学的人在学习上容易产生四种过失，这是施教的人需要了解的：求学的人学习失败的原因，或者是因为贪多，或者是因为所求偏狭，或者是因为态度轻浮，或者是因为畏难而止。这四点，都是由于求学的人的不同心思所造成的。施教的人要懂得求学的人的不同心思，才能帮助他们纠正这些过失。所谓善于施教，就是善于使求学的人能发挥其长处并纠正他们的过失。

【解析】

教师对学生除了普遍施教之外，还必须注意根据每个学生的具体情况进行个别教育。要善于发挥每个学生的长处，及时纠正他们的过失。

24.There are four common errors in education

There are four common errors in education which the teacher must be aware of. Some students try to learn too much, some learn too little, some learn things too easily and some are too easily discouraged. These four errors show that individuals differ in their mental endowments. When the teacher knows the different mental endowments, he can correct their mistakes. A teacher is but a man who tries to bring out the good and remedy the weaknesses of his students.

Book of Rituals · Record on Education

【 Commentary 】

A good teacher should modify his way of teaching to suit the special requirements of each student. It is important to give full play to students' talents and correct their defects in a timely manner.

25. 善教者，使人继其志

【原文】

善歌者，使人继其声；善教者，使人继其志。其言也约而达，微而臧，罕譬而喻，可谓继志矣。

《礼记·学记》

【释文】

善于唱歌的人，能够使人跟着他唱；善于施教的人，能够使人跟着他的思路去思考。教师的语言虽简要但十分畅达，虽含蓄但十分精妙，虽少用比喻但也明白易懂，这就可以说是善于使人跟着他的思路去思考。

【解析】

教师必须善于引导学生的思路，让他们能够认清求学的方向，沿着正确的道路去思考。教学中，教师的主导作用是不可轻忽的。

25.A good teacher makes other people carry out his ideas

A good singer makes men follow his tune, and a good teacher makes other people carry out his ideas. His words are concise but far-reaching, unpretentious, but deep; with few illustrations, but instructive. In this way, he may be said to perpetuate his ideas.

Book of Rituals · Record on Education

【 Commentary 】

A good teacher should be able to guide the students in right direction to study and think. The critical role that the teachers play in the process of teaching could not be overemphasized.

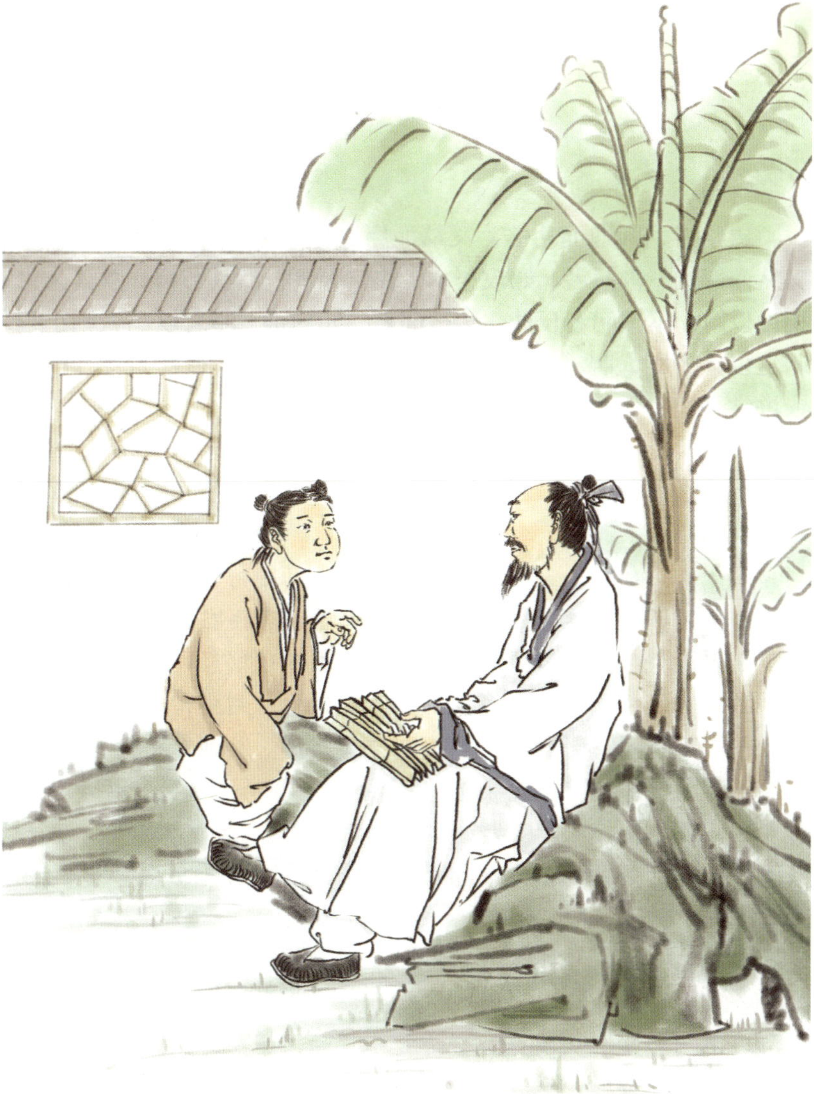

26. 善学者，师逸而功倍

【原文】

善学者，师逸而功倍，又从而庸之；不善学者，师勤而功半，又从而怨之。善问者，如攻坚木，先其易者，后其节目，及其久也，相说以解；不善问者反此。善待问者，如撞钟，叩之以小者则小鸣，叩之以大者则大鸣，待其从容，然后尽其声；不善答问者反此。此皆进学之道也。

《礼记·学记》

【释文】

善于学习的人，能使教师费力不大而功效倍增，并能感激教师教导有方；不善于学习的人，会使教师很劳苦而自己收效却很少，甚至还要埋怨教师。善于提问的人，像木工砍削坚硬的木头，先从容易的地方着手，再砍坚硬的部分，这样由易到难，时间长了问题也就解决了；不善于提问题的人却与此相反。教师对待提问的人，回答要针对具体对象，就像撞钟一样，撞钟的人用力小，钟声就小，撞钟的人用力大，钟声就大，如此从容地应对，问题就逐步解决了；不善于回答问题的人却与此相反。以上这些，都是有关增进学业的方法。

【解析】

在教与学中，仅有勤奋努力是不够的，还要讲究方法。教师怎样教，学生怎样学，学生怎样提问，教师怎样答问，前人积累了丰富的经验，值得我们认真研究和借鉴。

26.With a good student, the teacher does not have much to do and the results are double

With a good student, the teacher does not have much to do and the results are double, besides getting the student's respect. With a bad student, the teacher has to work hard and the results are only half of what is to be expected, besides getting complaints from the students. A good questioner proceeds like a man chopping wood — he begins at the easier end, attacking the knots last, and after a time the teacher and student talk together and the subject is explained. A bad questioner takes the opposite course. One who knows how to answer questions is like a group of bells. When you strike the big bell, the big one gives a great sound. When you strike the small bell, the small one gives a small sound. It is important, however, to allow time for its tone gradually to die out. One who does not know how to answer questions is exactly the opposite of this. These are all suggestions for the process of teaching and learning.

Book of Rituals · Record on Education

【 Commentary 】

In the process of teaching and learning, method is no less crucial than diligence. It is important to know how to study and raise questions as a student, and how to teach and answer questions as a teacher. The rich teaching and learning experiences in the past deserve our meticulous study.

27. 凡音者，生人心者也

【原文】

凡音者，生人心者也。情动于中，故形于声。声成文，谓之音。是故治世之音安以乐，其政和。乱世之音怨以怒，其政乖。亡国之音哀以思，其民困。声音之道，与政通矣。

《礼记·乐记》

【释文】

凡音乐，都出自人心。感情激荡在心中，于是就表现为声音。把声音组成动听的曲调，就叫作音乐。所以太平盛世的音乐安详而欢乐，反映了当时政治的和谐；混乱之世的音乐怨恨而愤怒，反映了当时政治的紊乱；亡国时候的音乐哀伤而忧思，反映了当时人民的困苦。由此看来，音乐的变化和政治的得失是相通的。

【解析】

音乐，包括弹奏的乐曲和歌唱的乐歌，都发自人的内心，是人的情感的抒发。任何时代，有怎样的政治，就会有怎样的音乐。也就是说，从当时流行的音乐中，可以看出政治的得失、社会的治乱、人心的向背与风俗的盛衰。

27.Music rises from the human heart

Music rises from the human heart. When the emotions are touched, they are expressed in sounds, and when the sounds take definite forms, we have music. Therefore, the music of a peaceful and prosperous country is quiet and joyous, and the government is orderly; the music of a country in turmoil shows dissatisfaction and anger, and the government is chaotic; and the music of a destroyed country shows sorrow and remembrance of the past, and the people are distressed. Therefore, we see music and government are directly connected with one another.

Book of Rituals · Record of Music

【 Commentary 】

Either a tune or a song is expressive of the internal feelings of human beings. Music is always expressive of time features. From the popular music in the past, we could tell the rise and fall of a government, a society and customs, and whether people supported their rulers or not at that time.

28. 乐者为同，礼者为异

【原文】

乐者为同，礼者为异。同则相亲，异则相敬，乐胜则流，礼胜则离。合情饰貌者礼乐之事也。

《礼记·乐记》

【释文】

乐的作用在于使尊卑上下关系协调，礼的作用在于使尊卑上下关系区分清楚。尊卑上下关系协调人们就会互相亲近感情融洽，尊卑上下关系区分清楚人们就会互相尊重恭敬有礼。过分强调乐会使人际关系过于随便而不知恭敬，过分强调礼又会使人际关系疏远而不相亲近。要使人际关系内心感情亲近融洽而外貌又互相尊重恭敬有礼，这就是礼乐恰当配合从而最有效地发挥其功效的事了。

28.Music unites, while rituals differentiate

Music unites, while rituals differentiate. From union comes mutual affection; from difference, mutual respect. If music prevails, the social structure becomes too amorphous, and if rituals predominate, social life becomes too cold. To bring the people's inner feelings and their external conduct into balance is the work of rituals and music.

Book of Rituals · Record of Music

【解析】

西周初年，周公制礼作乐，从此，礼与乐互相配合，发挥了巨大的社会功能。礼，主要指礼制，也就是尊卑上下的等级制度和秩序。乐，音乐，包括弹奏的乐曲和歌唱的乐歌。古人认为，礼主要讲人与人之间尊卑上下的区别，要求人们依礼而行，恭敬有礼。但仅有礼是不够的，还需要有乐。乐的主要功能是使人们心灵沟通，感情融洽。礼重在区别，乐重在和谐，礼与乐互相配合，就可以使社会既有序又和谐，从而达到天下太平。

【 Commentary 】

In the early years of the Western Zhou Dynasty, Duke Zhou instituted rituals and music. Ever since then, rituals and music have been mutually complemented each other and adopted by rulers to build a better society. Rituals mainly refer to the ritual institutions and reflect a hierarchical order in society. Music includes tunes and songs. Rituals imply that there is distinction between the superior and the inferior, thus, people should act in accordance with rituals. In addition, music is needed, for it is to facilitate a smooth communication and a harmonious relationship. Rituals emphasize difference and distinction. Similarity and union are the aims of music. The interaction of rituals and music will bring out a well-ordered, harmonious and peaceful society.

29. 乐由中出，礼自外作

【原文】

乐由中出，礼自外作。乐由中出故静，礼自外作故文。大乐必易，大礼必简。乐至则无怨，礼至则不争。揖让而治天下者，礼乐之谓也。

《礼记·乐记》

【释文】

乐是从内心发出的，礼则是从外在的行为中表现出来。由于乐从内心发出，所以人们心中就真诚平和；由于礼从外在的行为中表现出来，所以人们就恭敬谦让，文质彬彬。最高级的乐一定是平易的，最隆重的礼一定是简朴的。乐教深入人心，就会消除怨恨；礼教普遍施行，就会消除争斗。古代圣王之所以能以拱手揖让就把天下治理好，就是礼乐的功效。

【解析】

乐重在沟通人心，增进和谐；礼重在谦恭礼让，社会有序。两者互相配合，从而取得最大的社会功效。

29.Music comes from the inside, while rituals come from the outside

Music comes from the inside, while rituals come from the outside. Because music comes from the inside, it is characterized by quiet and calm. And because rituals come from the outside, they are characterized by elegancies of manner. Truly great music is always simple in movement, and truly great rituals are always simple in form. When good music prevails, there is no feeling of dissatisfaction. When proper rituals prevail, there is no strife and struggle. When we say that by mere bowing in salute the king can rule the world, we mean thereby the influence of rituals and music.

Book of Rituals · Record of Music

【 Commentary 】

Music is important to the communication of people as well as to harmonious interpersonal relationships. Rituals will help bring out a courteous atmosphere and a well-ordered society. They are mutually complementary, and should be given full play in the society.

30. 乐者，天地之和也；礼者，天地之序也

【原文】

乐者，天地之和也；礼者，天地之序也。和，故百物皆化；序，故群物皆别。

《礼记·乐记》

【释文】

所谓的乐，就像天地那样的和谐；所谓的礼，就像天地那样的有序。由于和谐，所以万物都能化生；由于有序，所以万物都千姿百态而秩序井然。

【解析】

古人认为，人类社会的乐和礼，都是效法天地，与天地有相同的规律。天地阴阳和谐从而滋生万物，乐正是天地阴阳和谐的反映；天地上下尊卑有序从而长养万物，礼正是天地上下尊卑有序的反映。

30.Music expresses the harmony of the universe, while rituals express the order of the universe

Music expresses the harmony of the universe, while rituals express the order of the universe. Through harmony all things are influenced, and through order all things have a proper place.

Book of Rituals · Record of Music

【 Commentary 】

According to the ancient Chinese, music and rituals were formed by following the universal laws. Music and rituals function in human society in the same way that the heaven and the earth do in nature. Music is the reflection of a harmonious union of the universe, and rituals are expressions of an orderly society.

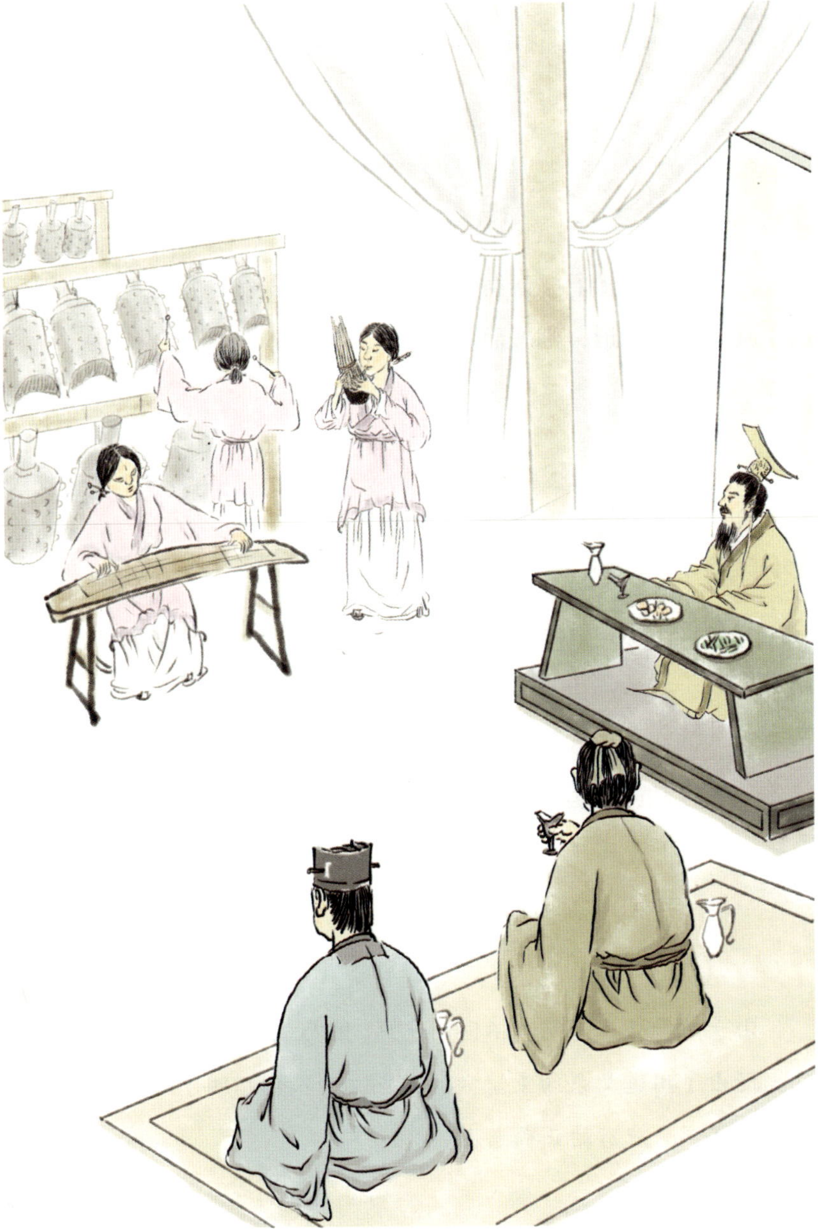

31. 乐者乐也

【原文】

    乐者，乐也。君子乐得其道，小人乐得其欲。以道制欲，则乐而不乱；以欲忘道，则惑而不乐。

《礼记·乐记》

【释文】

    音乐这个东西，是使人快乐的。但是君子感到快乐是因为从音乐中得到了道义，小人感到快乐是因为从音乐中满足了情欲。用道义来约束情欲，就会快乐而不至于迷乱；如果只为满足情欲而忘掉道义，就会使情感迷乱而得不到真正的快乐。

【解析】

    由于对待音乐有两种不同的态度，因而就产生两种不同的快乐。这里提出了用道义来约束情欲的观点，为人们指明了对待音乐以至一切感官享受应有的正确态度。

31.Music produces pleasure

Music produces pleasure. Moral men rejoice in attaining to the moral beings to be pursued; and vulgar men in obtaining the things that they desire. When the objects of desire are regulated by moral standards, there is pleasure without any disorder. When those objects lead to the forgetfulness of moral standards, there is delusion, and no joy.

Book of Rituals · Record of Music

【 Commentary 】

Two different attitudes about music will bring out two kinds of pleasures. In this entry, moral standards are highlighted to regulate evil desires. It points to a correct attitude that people should adopt toward music as well as other forms of sensual pleasure.

32. 乐统同，礼辨异

【原文】

　　乐也者，情之不可变者也；礼也者，理之不可易者也。乐统同，礼辨异，礼乐之说，管乎人情矣。

《礼记·乐记》

【释文】

　　我们所说的乐，所表达的是不可变易的恒常感情；我们所说的礼，所表达的是不可变易的恒常道理。乐是为了和同天下人心，礼是为了区别等级差异。礼和乐的学说，贯通了全部社会人情。

【解析】

　　乐和礼的功效，有不同的甚至相反的趋向。乐重在和，讲和同（使人心灵相通，关系和谐）；礼重在异，讲差异（使人遵守上下尊卑的等级秩序，恭敬有礼）。但在人类社会生活中，两者又是互补的，不可偏废。

32.Music embraces what all equally share; rituals distinguish the things in which men differ

Music is expressive of feelings that do not change; rituals demonstrate principles that do not alter. Music embraces what all equally share; rituals distinguish the things in which men differ. Therefore, the theory of music and rituals embraces human nature.

Book of Rituals · Record of Music

【 Commentary 】

As for the functions of music and rituals, there are similarities and differences. Music emphasizes harmony and aims to bring an amicable interpersonal relationship; whereas rituals value difference, and work for a hierarchical order. In human society, music and rituals are mutually complementary, and should be given equal emphasis.

33. 故歌之为言也，长言之也

【原文】

故歌之为言也，长言之也。说之，故言之；言之不足，故长言之；长言之不足，故嗟叹之；嗟叹之不足，故不知手之舞之，足之蹈之也。

《礼记·乐记》

【释文】

所以唱歌也是一种语言表达，只不过是拖长声音的语言表达罢了。心里高兴，就通过说话表达出来；说话还不足以表达心中的高兴，就拖长声音用歌唱来表达；拖长声音唱歌还不足以表达，那就加上咏叹；咏叹还不足以表达，那就情不自禁地手舞足蹈起来。

【解析】

音乐和舞蹈，同说话一样，都是为了表达内心感情，与他人交流沟通。不过，音乐所表达的感情，比一般的说话更为强烈罢了。

33.Singing means the prolonged expression of the words

Therefore, singing means the prolonged expression of the words. When the simple utterance of the words is not sufficient, there is the prolonged expression of them. When the prolonged expression is not sufficient, there come the sigh and exclamation. When these are insufficient, unconsciously there come the motions of the hands and the stamping of the feet.

Book of Rituals · Record of Music

【 Commentary 】

Music and dance function in a similar way as words do. Human beings need them to express internal emotions and communicate with each other. However, what is conveyed in musical forms is more intense than what is embodied in words.

34. 孝有三

【原文】

曾子曰："孝有三：大孝尊亲，其次弗辱，其下能养。"

《礼记·祭义》

【释文】

曾子说："孝有三等：第一等的孝是能光耀父母，使父母受人尊敬；第二等的孝是不使父母受辱，不使父母的名声受到玷污；第三等的孝是能够赡养父母，让父母衣食无忧。"

【解析】

曾子著《孝经》，阐发孔子的孝道。在这一则中，曾子认为，做子女的不仅要能赡养父母，更重要的是不使父母受辱，并进而能光宗耀祖。为此，从最低层次来说，做子女的要遵礼守法，不触犯刑律；从最高层次来说，做子女的要修身进德，建功立业，光耀门庭，以彰显父母。

34. There are three degrees of filial piety

Zengzi said, "There are three degrees of filial piety. The highest is to honor our parents; the second is not to disgrace them; and the lowest is being able to support them."

Book of Rituals · The Meaning of Sacrifices

【 Commentary 】

Zengzi illustrated the significance of filial piety in his *Book of Filial Piety*. According to Zengzi's words in this entry, sons and daughters should take care of their parents. More importantly, they should further honor their parents and the whole family. The minimum requirement is that sons and daughters should act according to rituals and laws. The demand at the highest level is that sons and daughters should elevate their moral standards and make achievements so as to honor their parents and the whole family.

35. 五者不遂，灾及于亲

【原文】

曾子曰："身也者，父母之遗体也。行父母之遗体，敢不敬乎？居处不庄，非孝也；事君不忠，非孝也；莅官不敬，非孝也；朋友不信，非孝也；战陈无勇，非孝也。五者不遂，灾及于亲，敢不敬乎？"

《礼记·祭义》

【释文】

曾子说："自己的身体，是父母给予的。用父母给予的身体来做事，怎敢不小心谨慎呢？日常起居不庄重，就是不孝；为君主做事而不尽心尽力，就是不孝；担任公职而不严肃认真，就是不孝；对朋友不讲诚信，就是不孝；临阵作战不勇敢向前，就是不孝。这五个方面做不到，不仅自己遭殃，还会殃及父母，怎敢不小心谨慎呢？"

【解析】

曾子认为，一个人，侍奉君主要尽心尽力，担任公职要严肃认真，同人交往要诚实守信。总之，立身行事，都要严于律己，不使父母受辱，进而能彰显父母，这样做，才称得上孝。否则，就是不孝。

35.If he fails in these five duties, the evil of the disgrace will reach his parents

Zengzi said, "The body is that which has been transmitted to us by our parents; dare any one allow himself to be irreverent in the employment of their legacy? If a man is not grave in his own house and privacy, he is not filial; if a man is not loyal in serving his ruler, he is not filial; if a man is not reverent in discharging his office duties, he is not filial; if a man is not sincere with friends, he is not filial; if a man is not brave on the battle field, he is not filial. If he fails in these five duties, the evil of the disgrace will reach his parents; dare he but reverently attend to them?"

Book of Rituals · The Meaning of Sacrifices

【 Commentary 】

According to Zengzi, a man should be loyal in serving his ruler, reverent in discharging the duties of office and sincere with his friends. He must be strict with himself. His words and deeds must honor his parents and this is what is in accordance with filial piety.

36. 此之谓礼终

　　父母爱之，嘉而弗忘。父母恶之，惧而无怨。父母有过，谏而不逆。父母既没，必求仁者之粟以祀之。此之谓礼终。

《礼记·祭义》

【释文】

　　父母喜爱自己，自己就高兴地永远铭记在心。父母不喜欢自己，自己就戒惧反省而无怨言。父母有了过失，自己就婉言规劝而不和他们顶撞。父母去世，从仁君那里取得俸禄从而依礼举行祭祀。这就叫作终身依礼奉行孝道。

【解析】

　　这也是曾子说的话。曾子认为，父母从生到死，做子女的都要依礼奉行孝道。这是终身之事，而不是一时之事。

36.The fulfillment of a filial son's proper services

When his parents love him, the filial son should be happy and not allow himself to forget them; when they hate him, the filial son should fear but feel no resentment; when they commit faults, the filial son should admonish them but not withstand them; when they are dead, the filial son should ask the help only of the good to obtain the grain for the sacrifice — this is what is called the fulfillment of a filial son's proper services.

Book of Rituals · The Meaning of Sacrifices

【 Commentary 】

This entry was a quote from Zengzi. According to him, sons and daughters should maintain the ideals of filial piety and act in accordance with the rituals. It is a lifelong duty.

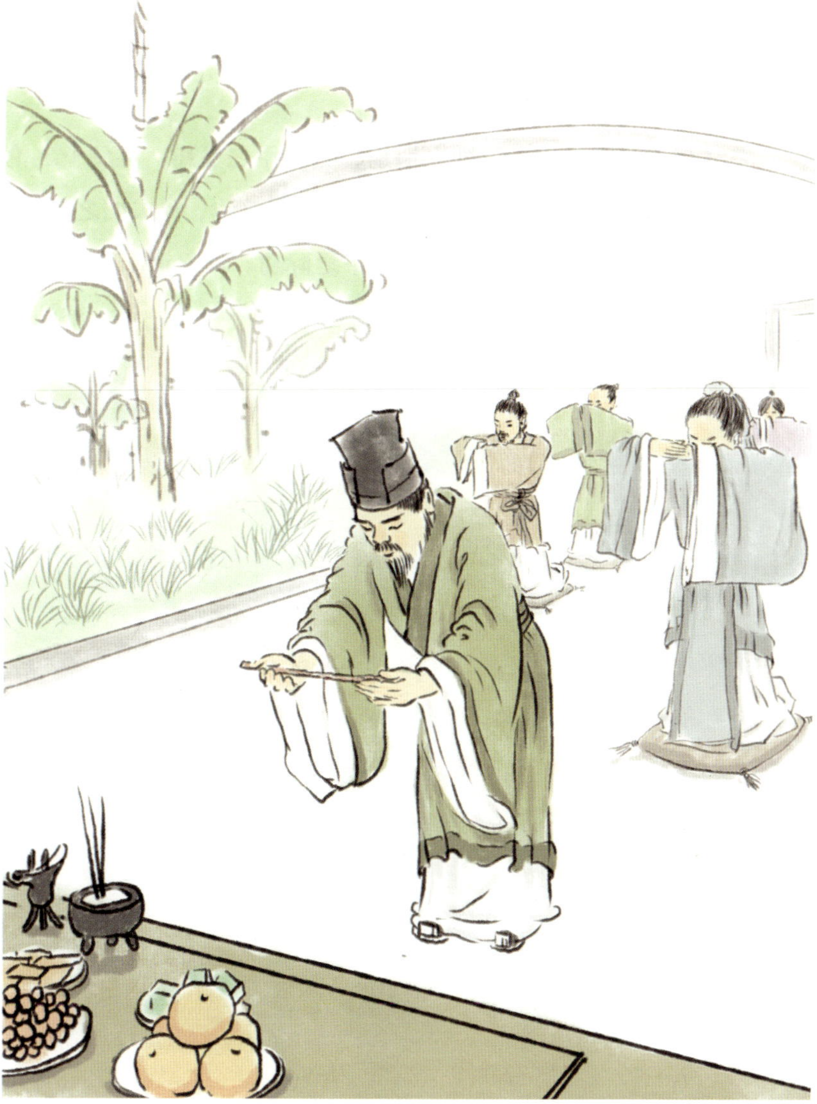

37. 祭有十伦

【原文】

夫祭有十伦焉：见事鬼神之道焉，见君臣之义焉，见父子之伦焉，见贵贱之等焉，见亲疏之杀焉，见爵赏之施焉，见夫妇之别焉，见政事之均焉，见长幼之序焉，见上下之际焉。此之谓十伦。

《礼记·祭统》

【释文】

祭祀有十种伦理方面的意义：第一是体现事奉鬼神、天人沟通的道理，第二是体现君礼臣忠的道理，第三是体现父慈子孝的道理，第四是体现贵贱有别的道理，第五是体现亲疏有别的道理，第六是体现爵赏依礼施行的道理，第七是体现夫妇有别的道理，第八是体现政事均平的道理，第九是体现长幼有序的道理，第十是体现上下和谐的道理。这就是祭祀的十种伦理方面的意义。

37.In sacrifice there is a recognition that belongs to ten relationships

In sacrifice there is a recognition that belongs to ten relationships: the method of serving spiritual beings, the moral beings between ruler and subject, the relation between father and son, the degrees of the noble and mean, the distance gradually increasing between relatives, the bestowment of rank and reward, the separate duties of husband and wife, impartiality in government affairs, the order to be observed between old and young, and the boundaries of high and low. These are what are called the different duties in the ten relationships.

Book of Rituals · Summary of Sacrifices

【解析】

　　祭祀是一种礼仪，而礼仪则是礼制的反映。在礼仪中，明确体现了上下尊卑的等级制度和秩序，以及相应的伦理道德。在古代，君礼臣忠，父慈子孝，兄友弟恭，夫妻相敬，朋友有信，这一类的伦理道德，在各种礼仪、礼俗中不断得到强化和发展，其内涵也随着社会的发展而不断更新。其中一些未能跟上社会发展的部分，已被人们抛弃，而另一些优秀的部分，今天仍然值得我们继承和发扬。

【 Commentary 】

Sacrifices actually follow a code of ceremonies that reflect ritual regulations. The boundaries of high and low, the order to be observed between old and young, a hierarchical system and moral standards are all clarified in rituals. In ancient China, rulers were respectful and subjects were loyal; father loves his son and son was filial; brothers loved each other; husband and wife respected each other; friends were trustful. Rituals and ceremonial usages of society were developed and reinforced along with the time vicissitude. There were also changes in the definitions and meanings of certain ritual rules. We should forsake the rules that fail to keep pace with the times, and carry forward those that will contribute to a better society.

38. 入其国，其教可知也

【原文】

孔子曰："入其国，其教可知也。其为人也，温柔敦厚，《诗》教也；疏通知远，《书》教也；广博易良，《乐》教也；洁静精微，《易》教也；恭俭庄敬，《礼》教也；属辞比事，《春秋》教也。"

《礼记·经解》

【释文】

孔子说："进入一个国家，只要看看民众的素质就可以知道这个国家对民众的教化是怎样的了。观察他们的为人及待人接物，如果是温和柔顺而又纯朴忠厚，那是用《诗》教化的结果；如果是知识通达并了解古代之事，那是用《书》教化的结果；如果是心胸广阔坦荡而又平易善良，那是用《乐》教化的结果；如果是思虑洁静而又洞察细微，那是用《易》教化的结果；如果是恭敬俭约而又庄重谨慎，那是用《礼》教化的结果；如果是善于连缀文辞排比事实从而判断是非，那是用《春秋》教化的结果。"

38.When entering a country, one gets to know the type of education on its people

Confucius remarked, "When entering a country, one gets to know the type of education on its people. When its people are gentle and simple, it shows the teaching of the *Book of Poetry*. When they are broad-minded and acquainted with the past, it shows the teaching of the *Book of History*. When they are generous and show a good disposition, it shows the teaching of the *Book of Music*. When they are quiet and thoughtful, and show a sharp power of observation, it shows the teaching of the *Book of Changes*. When they are humble and respectful and frugal in their habits, it shows the teaching of the *Ceremonial Etiquette*. When they are cultivated in their speech, ready with expressions and analogies, it shows the teaching of the *Spring and Autumn*."

Book of Rituals · Education on the Six Classics

【解析】

　　早在中国的战国时代，《诗三百》《尚书》《周易》《乐经》《仪礼》《春秋》这六部书，就被人们称为"经"。"经"的意思是常，表示这"六经"人们应当常读常行，因为它们的思想内容是指导人们做人做事的最高典范。古人十分重视用"六经"来教化民众，培养人才。时至今日，研读"六经"对我们继承和弘扬优秀的思想文化传统，仍有积极意义。

【 Commentary 】

In the period of the Warring States, the *Six Classics*, namely the *Book of Poetry*, the *Book of History*, the *Book of Music*, the *Book of Changes*, the *Ceremonial Etiquette* and the *Spring and Autumn*, were already regarded as "canons." The Chinese character *jing* (canon) originally means "frequently," "regularly," or "customary," and it implies that reading these six books became a daily practice at that time. The core values in the *Six Classics* were the highest standards for the code of conduct in ancient China. Therefore, they were greatly valued and used by the rulers to cultivate the people and train the professionals. It is still of great significance to study the *Six Classics* and to spread the excellent culture to the world.

39. 安上治民，莫善于礼

【原文】

孔子曰："安上治民，莫善于礼。"

《礼记·经解》

【释文】

孔子说："安定在上位者的地位，治理在下位的民众，没有比礼更好的了。"

【解析】

礼的核心内容是上下尊卑的等级制度和秩序，以及相应的伦理道德。礼的产生，标志着人类文明社会的开始。孔子认为，礼的施行，应以保持中道与和谐为贵。上下尊卑之间，人与人之间，应当互敬互爱，建立良好的伦理道德和秩序，使社会日趋和谐稳定。

39. There is nothing better than the rituals for the maintaining of authority and the governing of the people

Confucius remarked, "There is nothing better than the rituals for the maintaining of authority and the governing of the people."

Book of Rituals · Education on the *Six Classics*

【 Commentary 】

The core of the rituals is relevant to a hierarchical order, the ethics and the moral beings. The formation of the rituals signifies the beginning of a civilized society. According to Confucius, the practice of the rituals should follow the rule that the moral beings and the central harmony must be maintained. The superiors and the inferiors should respect and love each other. A sound system of ethics and morals will bring out a stable and harmonious society.

40. 古之为政，爱人为大

【原文】

古之为政，爱人为大。

《礼记·哀公问》

【释文】

古人管理政务治理国家，把爱人看得最重要。

【解析】

这是孔子对鲁哀公所问的回答。孔子认为，爱人，也就是爱别人（主要是爱民众），是在上位的执政者最重要的政治原则和政治道德。

40.In the practice of government in ancient times, loving the people is considered as the first thing

In the practice of government in ancient times, loving the people is considered as the first thing.

Book of Rituals · Questions from the Duke Ai

【 Commentary 】

This is Confucius' answer to one of Duke Ai's questions. According to Confucius, loving the people, or loving the general public, is the most important political principle and moral standard for those in authority.

41. 贵乎天道

【原文】

公曰："敢问君子何贵乎天道也？"孔子对曰："贵其'不已'，如日月东西相从而不已也，是天道也；不闭其久，是天道也；无为而物成，是天道也；已成而明，是天道也。"

《礼记·哀公问》

【释文】

鲁哀公问道："请问君子为什么看重天道呢？"孔子回答说："看重它的运行永不止息，就好像日月的东升西落永不止息，这就是天道；看重它的畅通无阻而且保持永久，这就是天道；看重它任其自然而万物皆成，这就是天道；看重它的万物皆成而且清楚明白，这就是天道。"

【解析】

古代中国人追求天人合一。他们认为，天道是公正、公平、正直和无私的，是无比刚健永不止息的。人道应当效法天道。《周易》说：天道的运行无比刚健而永不停息，君子应以天道为楷模，奋发图强而永不停息。

41.Lay stress on the laws of God

Duke Ai asked, "May I ask why the gentleman lays such stress on the laws of God?" Confucius remarked, "The gentleman lays such stress upon God's laws, because it is eternal. For instance, the sun and the moon eternally follow one another in their courses — that is God's law. Life in this universe never stops and continues forever — that is God's law. Things are made in a complete manner without any effort or interference — that is God's law. When things are made in a complete manner, the universe is illuminated — that is God's law."

Book of Rituals · Questions from the Duke Ai

【 Commentary 】

The "harmony of man with nature" is a long-cherished pursuit of the ancient Chinese people. The God's laws are just, fair, correct and impartial. And they are powerful and eternal. Therefore, human beings on earth should follow the laws of God. According to the *Book of Changes*, the movement of heaven is full of power and constant. Thus the gentleman should model himself on it and make himself strong and untiring.

42. 礼也者，理也

【原文】

子曰："礼也者，理也；乐也者，节也。君子无理不动，无节不作。"

《礼记·仲尼燕居》

【释文】

孔子说："所谓礼，就是要讲道理；所谓乐，就是要有节制。不合理的事君子不做，无节制的事君子不做。"

【解析】

礼乐虽然都表现为人们外在的行为，但礼乐的基础在道义，在人们内在的道德修养，要求人们做任何事都要合理而不悖逆，有节而不逾矩。只有这样，礼乐才能真正起到约束和规范人们行为的作用。

42.Rituals are reasons

Confucius remarked, "Rituals are instructions of reasons; music is the limitation. A gentleman will never move without reasons and will do nothing without knowing its limitation."

Book of Rituals · Zhongni stays idle at home

【 Commentary 】

Rituals and music seem to associate with external conduct of human beings, yet they are formed to elevate the internal moral standards. With rituals and music, human beings are required to act in a reasonable and appropriate manner. In so doing, rituals and music can function to regularize the actions of human beings.

43. 君子之道，辟则坊与

【原文】

子言之："君子之道，辟则坊与，坊民之所不足者也。大为之坊，民犹逾之。故君子礼以坊德，刑以坊淫，命以坊欲。"

《礼记·坊记》

【释文】

孔子说："在上位的君子治理民众的办法，打个比方来说，就好像为了防止河水泛滥而筑起堤坝，以防止人们出现过失。虽然严加防范，但还是有人犯规越轨。所以君子用礼教来防止人们道德上的缺失，用刑罚来防止人们邪恶行为的产生，用政令来防止人们贪婪欲望的膨胀。"

【解析】

孔子认为，在日常社会生活中，有人会做缺德甚至悖逆的事，需要预先防范。大力加强礼教、乐教，正确运用刑罚、政令，都是防范的有效手段。

43.The moral laws that a gentleman follows can be likened to dykes

Confucius remarked, "The moral laws that a gentleman follows can be likened to dykes. They serve to guard against people who are morally deficient. The precautions may be carried out on a large scale, people still transgress them. Hence, a gentleman will depend on rituals to complement moral deficiency; on punishments to guard against carnal desires; and on decrees to guard against evil desires."

Book of Rituals · Record of Dykes

【 Commentary 】

According to Confucius, precautions are needed to guard against the people who are morally deficient or rebellious. It is important to lay great emphasis on the education of rituals and music. Effective means include punishments and decrees.

44. 天命之谓性

【原文】

天命之谓性，率性之谓道，修道之谓教。

《礼记·中庸》

【释文】

人的自然禀赋叫作"性"，顺着本性去做叫作"道"，按照"道"的原则修身养性叫作"教"。

【解析】

这句意思是说，中庸（中和）之道原本就存在于天赋的本性中，为人性之所固有，顺着本性行事，就是正道、达道——中庸（中和）之道。人们据此修养自己和教化他人，就叫作"教"。人们应当重视本性中的本然之善（执中守正，折中致和，行止有度，因时制宜），自觉地去保有它，养护它。

44.The ordinance of God is what we call the law of our being

The ordinance of God is what we call the law of our being. To fulfill the law of our being is what we call the moral law. The moral law when reduced to a system is what we call religion.

Book of Rituals · Central Harmony

【 Commentary 】

The universal moral law (find the central balance in moral nature) is an inherent part of human nature. The right and universal way to fulfill the law of our being is to act according to our nature. To reduce the self-cultivation and the teaching of others to a system is what we call religion. We should treasure and preserve this natural goodness (maintain the central point and guard the upright, keep the central balance and fulfill the moral sense, act in accordance with conduct and time).

45. 中为天下之大本，和为天下之达道

【原文】

中也者，天下之大本也；和也者，天下之达道也。

《礼记·中庸》

【释文】

执中守正，是天下一切情感和道理的根本；折中致和，是天下一切事物的普遍原则。

【解析】

《中庸》从人的性情来阐释"中庸（中和）"之道。当"喜怒哀乐"未发之时，人的性情自然是中正不偏的，这就是"中"（是先天的禀赋）；而一旦接触了外物，有了"喜怒哀乐"之情，但抒发出来都合乎"执两用中"，并且"无过无不及"，这就是"和"，是后天教化所获。可见，"中庸（中和）"之道是天下一切情感和道理的根本，也是天下一切事物的普遍原则。

45.Moral being is the great reality existence; moral order is the universal law in the world

Our true self or moral being is the great reality existence, and moral order is the universal law in the world.

Book of Rituals · Central Harmony

【 Commentary 】

The book *Zhongyong* (Central Harmony, or The Universal Order) explains "moral being" and "moral order" from the perspective of human emotions. When "happiness, anger, sadness or joy" is not generated, a man is true and impartial, and this is what "moral being (a natural endowment)" means; when those emotions are produced upon various occasions, a moral man can take the two extremes of negative and positive, and apply the mean of the two extremes. Moreover, he will either go beyond the mark, or not come up to it. And this is "moral order" which can be acquired through education and cultivation. Thus, the universal moral order is the basis of all emotions and principles. It is also the fundamental law for everything in the world.

46. 君子而时中

【原文】

君子之中庸也，君子而时中。

《礼记·中庸》

【释文】

君子之所以总是按中庸行事，是因为君子总能因时制宜按照当时情况做到执中守正，无过无不及。

【解析】

道德高尚的"君子"，因为有君子之德，所以能"时中"，即"随时以处中"。也就是说，君子总能因时制宜，根据不同时间、不同地点、不同情况、不同条件，或执中守正，或折中致和，从而总能处在"不偏不倚""无过无不及"的中正位置上。因此，君子每时每刻都能持守中道，这是君子的操守。

46.The moral man unceasingly cultivates his moral being

The moral man's life is an exemplification of the universal order, because he is a moral person who unceasingly cultivates his true self or moral being.

Book of Rituals · Central Harmony

【 Commentary 】

A "moral man" with high moral standards unceasingly cultivates his true self or moral being. In other words, a moral man acts in line with time, places, conditions and scenarios; he maintains the central point and guards the upright, keeps the central balance and fulfills the moral sense; he situates himself in an impartial position, neither going beyond the mark nor coming up to it. Hence, he can always maintain the universal moral order, for it is the integrity of a moral man.

47. 中庸其至矣乎

【原文】

中庸其至矣乎！

《礼记·中庸》

【释文】

中庸之道大概是最高的德行了吧！

【解析】

孔子认为，中庸之德是最高的境界，但一般人难于执守，往往不是"过"就是"不及"，这是由于教化缺失所致，因此孔子发出深深的感叹。

47.To find and get into the true central balance of our moral being

To find and get into the true central balance of our moral being, i.e. our true moral ordinary self, that indeed is the highest human attainment.

Book of Rituals · Central Harmony

【 Commentary 】

According to Confucius, the highest human attainment is to find and get into the true central balance of our moral being. However, most of us will either go beyond the mark, or not come up to it. And this fact results from the lack of education. No wonder Confucius sighed so sympathetically.

48. 执其两端，用其中于民

【原文】

执其两端，用其中于民。

《礼记·中庸》

【释文】

舜善于掌握"过"与"不及"两端的情况及方方面面的情况，通过折中调和，确定中正恰当的决策，而施行于老百姓。

【解析】

"执其两端，用其中于民"，是说凡事都先弄清楚事物或问题两个极端（或对立的两个方面）的情况，弄清楚事物或问题方方面面的情况，然后通过折中调和，找出"中正""中和"的办法，运用到民众身上，这就叫作"执两用中"，"折中致和"，无"过"也无"不及"，是中庸之道作为方法论的精髓。

48.Taking the two extremes of negative and positive, and applying the mean in the dealing with people

Taking the two extremes of negative and positive, he (Shun) applied the mean between the two extremes in his judgment, employment and dealings with people.

Book of Rituals · Central Harmony

【 Commentary 】

This line tells us to take into consideration of the opposite sides or the two extremes of a problem, and also examine a problem from all angles. After that, we need to adopt the "mean measures" in accordance with the "moral order." This is what is called "maintaining the central point and guarding the upright," or "keeping the central balance and fulfilling the moral sense." There is either "going beyond the mark," or "not coming up to it." It is the essence of the universal moral order.

49. 君子和而不流，中立而不倚

【原文】

君子和而不流，强哉矫！中立而不倚，强哉矫！国有道，不变塞焉，强哉矫！国无道，至死不变，强哉矫！

《礼记·中庸》

【释文】

品德高尚的君子性情平和但不随波逐流，这才是真正的坚强啊！持守中正而不偏不倚，这才是真正的坚强啊！国家政治清平时不改变志向，这才是真正的坚强啊！国家政治黑暗时坚持操守，宁死不变，这才是真正的坚强啊！

【解析】

孔子弟子子路一向好勇逞强，孔子针对子路之问，提出"北方之强"与"南方之强"加以辨析，并告诉子路，应当"和而不流"，"中立而不倚"，任何时候都不改变原有的"中正""中和"的操守，这才是真正的"强"。孔子曾说，君子有勇而无义就会搞叛乱，勇敢却不懂礼就会莽撞乱来。认为子路之"勇"，要用"礼义"来节制，回归中庸之道。

49.The moral man is independent without any bias

Wherefore the man with the true force of moral character is one who is easy and accommodating and yet without weakness or indiscrimination. How unflinchingly firm he is in his strength! He is independent without any bias. How unflinchingly firm he is in his strength! When there is moral social order in the country, if he enters public life he does not change from what he was when in retirement. How unflinchingly firm he is in his strength! When there is no moral social order in the country he holds on his way without changing even unto death. How unflinchingly firm he is in his strength!

Book of Rituals · Central Harmony

【 Commentary 】

Zilu, one of Confucius' disciples, was so fond of parading his valor and superiority. This entry is actually the answer provided by Confucius to a question from Zilu. Confucius thought, a moral man should be "easy and accommodating and yet without weakness or indiscrimination," and "independent without any bias." He must unswervingly maintain his integrity: "seeking the central point in moral being," or "abiding by the universal moral order." This is what is called "unflinchingly firm strength." A gentleman who has valor, but is without knowledge and love of what is right, is likely to commit a crime. Confucius thought, the valor from Zilu should not be overdeveloped, and only "knowledge and love of what is right" can bring him back to the right track of moral order.

50. 夫孝者，善继人之志，善述人之事

【原文】

夫孝者，善继人之志，善述人之事者也。

《礼记·中庸》

【释文】

所谓孝的最高境界，就是要（像周武王和周公那样）善于继承前人的遗志，善于完成前人所未完成的事业。

【解析】

武王继承文王遗志，伐纣灭殷，建立周王朝。武王死后，周公辅佐成王，东征平叛，分封诸侯，制礼作乐，天下大治，又一次证明了道用之广大。周公制礼作乐，是围绕着宗法制进行的。在当时，实行分封制、宗法制，对巩固王权，促进统一，维护社会稳定，恢复和发展生产，具有进步意义和积极作用。而周公的制礼作乐，则是围绕着宗法制，建立起一系列的社会、政治制度，以及与之适应的一系列的道德伦理规范和文化教育制度。这是当时社会进一步走向文明的重要标志。

50.True filial piety consists in carrying out the unfinished work of our forefathers and transmitting their achievements to posterity

Now, true filial piety consists in successfully carrying out the unfinished work of our forefathers and transmitting their achievements to posterity.

Book of Rituals · Central Harmony

【 Commentary 】

The Emperor Wu carried out the unfinished work of his father the Emperor Wen, and overthrew the Emperor Zhou of the Yin Dynasty and established the Zhou Dynasty. After the Emperor Wu's death, the Emperor Cheng, assisted by the Duke Zhou, put down the rebellion in the east, granted the titles and territories to the nobles, recreated the ceremonial rituals and music, and furthered the cause of peace and prosperity, all of which demonstrated the moral order is universally applicable. At that time, the establishment of patriarchal clan system and the enfeoffment system were of great historical significance, because it played an active role in consolidating the monarchy, promoting reunification, maintaining social stability, restoring and developing production. Based on patriarchal clan system, Duke Zhou drew up the ceremonial rituals and music, and set up a series of social and political systems, ethical regulations, cultural and educational systems. This was an important sign that a more civilized society was being formed.

51. 天下之五达道

君臣也，父子也，夫妇也，昆弟也，朋友之交也；五者，天下之达道也。

《礼记·中庸》

【释文】

君臣、父子、夫妇、兄弟、朋友之间的交往，这五项是天下人普遍的伦常关系。

【解析】

儒家主张父慈子孝，兄友弟恭，君臣相得，夫妻相敬，朋友有信，认为这是社会上最普遍的伦理道德。

51.The five duties of universal obligation

The duties are those between ruler and subject; between father and son; between husband and wife; between elder and younger brothers; and those in the intercourse between friends. These are the five duties of universal obligation.

Book of Rituals · Central Harmony

【 Commentary 】

Confucius remarked, a good father loves his children and a good son honors his father; the elder and the younger brothers should always be earnest to each other; let the ruler treat his subject with honor and the subject serve the ruler with loyalty; the husband and wife should always maintain the same careful respect; in the intercourse with friends, he should always be sincere and truthful. These are the moral duties of universal obligations.

52. 极高明而道中庸

【原文】

礼仪三百，威仪三千，待其人然后行。……故君子尊德性而道问学，致广大而尽精微，极高明而道中庸。

《礼记·中庸》

【释文】

礼仪三百条，具体仪节多达三千条，都有待于贤人出来才能施行。……因此君子诚心尊崇天赋的德性也努力从事后天的学习，广泛追求极其广博的知识也深入钻研极其精微的学问，达到极其高明的境界也遵循不偏不倚的中庸之道。

【解析】

礼仪节文众多，都要依靠贤人来施行。圣人能效法天道，参与天地的化育。君子就应以圣人为榜样，尊重那天赋的德性而又努力问道求学，使学问既广博又精深，诚心诚意遵循中庸之道而行，从而达到最高明的境界。

52. Seek to understand the highest things, and live a plain, ordinary life in accordance with the moral order

Three hundred rules of rituals and three thousand rules of conducts await the worthy men before they are carried out in practice. … Wherefore the moral man, while honoring the greatness and power of his moral nature, yet does not neglect inquiry and pursuit of knowledge. While widening the extent of his knowledge, he yet seeks to attain utmost accuracy in the minute details. While seeking to understand the highest things, he yet lives a plain, ordinary life in accordance with the moral order.

Book of Rituals · Central Harmony

【 Commentary 】

It is the worthy men who are depended upon for the practice of various rules of rituals and conducts. The ancient men with perfect nature followed the universal order and influenced the forces of creation of the universe. A moral man should take the sages as role models and depend on both intuition and education, so that he could widen the extent of his knowledge and attain utmost accuracy in the minute details. As long as he acts in accordance with the universal moral order, he will reach the realm of the highest excellence.

53. 温故而知新，敦厚以崇礼

温故而知新，敦厚以崇礼。

《礼记·中庸》

【释文】

温习已有的知识从而获得新知识，以道德的淳厚来崇奉礼仪法度。

【解析】

温习历史，继承传统，是为了获取新知，开创未来。修养身心，增强道德，是为了修明法度，治国安邦。

53.Going over what he has already acquired, he keeps adding to it new knowledge

Going over what he has already acquired, he keeps adding to it new knowledge. Earnest and simple, he respects and obeys the laws and usages of social life.

Book of Rituals · Central Harmony

【 Commentary 】

To acquire new knowledge and make achievements in future, we need to draw experience from the history and carry on the tradition. To formulate impartial laws and secure a good government, we need to nurture and cultivate our body and mind, so as to improve our moral standards.

54. 仁者，天下之表也

【原文】

　　子言之："仁者，天下之表也；义者，天下之制也；报者，天下之利也。"

　　　　　　　　　　　　　　　　　　　　《礼记·表记》

【释文】

　　孔子说："仁是天下之人的仪表，义是天下之人的准则，报施是天下之人的利益。"

【解析】

　　仁者爱人，仁爱之心应当表现在容颜上，表现在言谈举止中；义者宜也，义的意思是合理，人的行为应当符合道义，道义是人们行为的准则；礼尚往来，礼重报施，人人互敬互爱，人人都能从中获利受益。在孔子看来，仁、义、礼、利，其内容和精神是相通的。

54.Humanity is the pattern for everything under heaven

Confucius remarked, "Humanity is the pattern for everything under heaven; honor and duty is the law for everything under heaven; and reciprocations are the profit for everything under heaven."

Book of Rituals · Record on Example

【 Commentary 】

Moral men with the spirit of humanity love human beings. Kindness and love can be felt from facial expression, words and deeds. Honor and duty is the principle of human conduct. Courtesy requires a return of visits received. Reciprocations are the features of rituals. Mutual benefits are produced between people who respect and love each other. According to Confucius, humanity, honor, duty, rituals and profit are all intimately related.

55. 君子之接如水

【原文】

子曰："君子之接如水，小人之接如醴；君子淡以成，小人甘以坏。"

《礼记·表记》

【释文】

孔子说："君子交友平淡得好像清水，小人交友甘甜得好像甜酒；君子交友虽然平淡得好像清水，但情感相通必能相辅相成，小人交友虽然甘甜得好像甜酒，但情感不通日久必然败坏。"

【解析】

君子同人交往，心意真诚，表里如一，关系看似平淡，但由于心灵相通，所以能相辅相成。小人同人交往，往往甜言蜜语，逢迎巴结，看似亲密无比，心灵实不相通，不但友谊不真，还会败坏事情。

55.The intercourse of moral men may be compared to water

Confucius remarked, "The intercourse of moral men may be compared to water, and that of vulgar men, to sweet wine. The moral men seem insipid, but they help to perfection; the vulgar men seem sweet, but they lead to ruin."

Book of Rituals · Record on Example

【 Commentary 】

A moral man will be sincere in the association with other people, and his deeds accord with his words. It seems insipid but lasts long. A vulgar man will coax others with delusive promises. It seems sweet, but their friendship is not built upon faith.

56. 口惠而实不至，怨灾及其身

【原文】

子曰："口惠而实不至，怨灾及其身。是故君子与其有诺责也，宁有已怨。"

《礼记·表记》

【释文】

孔子说："口头上许给人家好处而实际上又做不到，怨恨或灾祸就会降临到他身上。所以，君子与其遭受不能兑现承诺的责难，还不如承受拒绝承诺的埋怨。"

【解析】

君子的为人，应当诚实守信，言行一致，说到做到，做不到的事不要轻易许诺或承诺。

56.Dissatisfaction and calamity will come to him whose lip-kindness is not followed by the corresponding deeds

Confucius remarked, "Dissatisfaction and calamity will come to him whose lip-kindness is not followed by the corresponding deeds. Therefore, a moral man will rather incur the resentment arising from his refusal than the charge of promising and then not fulfilling."

Book of Rituals · Record on Example

【 Commentary 】

A moral man should always be honest and truthful. What he says and does should correspond with what is on his mind. He must be true in words and resolute in deeds. He should not promise to do what is beyond his capability.

57. 情欲信，辞欲巧

子曰："情欲信，辞欲巧。"

《礼记·表记》

孔子说："感情要力求真实，说话要讲究技巧。"

君子待人，感情必须真诚，但说话则需要顾及效果，比如根据情况，有时需要委婉含蓄。

57.What is required in feeling is sincerity, what is required in words is refinement

Confucius remarked, "What is required in feeling is sincerity. What is required in words is refinement."

Book of Rituals · Record on Example

【 Commentary 】

A gentleman is sincere with others, but he should also be careful to use tactful language, for sometimes implicit remarks are more appropriate.

58. 好贤如《缁衣》

【原文】

子曰："好贤如《缁衣》，恶恶如《巷伯》，则爵不渎而民作愿，刑不试而民咸服。"

《礼记·缁衣》

【释文】

孔子说："在上位的君子如果能够像《缁衣》那首诗所说的那样尊重贤人，像《巷伯》那首诗所说的那样厌恶坏人，官爵就不会滥封而民风就会淳厚，刑罚不用施行而百姓自然顺服。"

【解析】

执政者如果执政为公，尊贤疾恶，爱憎分明，赏罚严明，政风与民风都会变得淳厚。

58. The worthy is favored as what is in the *Black Robes*

Confucius remarked, "When the worthy is favored as what is in the *Black Robes*, and the evil is hated as in the *Xiangbo*, the people are stimulated to be good without the frequent conferring of rank, and they are all obedient to the orders without the use of punishments."

Book of Rituals · Black Robes

【 Commentary 】

If the men in authority are impartial, respect the worthy and attack the evil, know clearly what to love and what to hate, both the work style and the people will become simple and unspoiled.

59. 子以爱之，则民亲之

【原文】

　　子曰："故君民者，子以爱之，则民亲之；信以结之，则民不倍；恭以莅之，则民有孙心。"

《礼记·缁衣》

【释文】

　　孔子说："所以统治百姓的人，如能像爱护子女一样爱护百姓，百姓就会亲近他；如能用诚信之心去团结百姓，百姓就不会背叛他；如能用恭敬的态度去对待百姓，百姓就会产生顺从之心。"

【解析】

　　爱民如子，用诚信之心和恭敬的态度去对待百姓，这些都是统治者基本的政治道德。

59.If the ruler loves the people as his sons, they will feel to him as a parent

Confucius remarked, "If the ruler loves the people as his sons, they will feel to him as a parent; if he binds them by his good faith, they will not betray him; if he presides over them with courtesy, their hearts are docile to him."

Book of Rituals · Black Robes

【 Commentary 】

Those in authority must treat the people with respect and love them the way they love their own children. This is the fundamental requirement for a ruler of a country.

60. 民以君为心，君以民为体

【原文】

子曰："民以君为心，君以民为体。……心以体全，亦以体伤；君以民存，亦以民亡。"

《礼记·缁衣》

【释文】

孔子说："民众把君主当作自己的心脏，君主把民众当作自己的身体。……心脏由于身体安全而得到保全，心脏也会由于身体遭到损伤而受到损伤；君主由于民众的拥护而存在，君主也会由于民众的反对而灭亡。"

【解析】

这是一个绝妙的比喻。君主如心，民众如体，心随体而存亡。这就告诉君主，民众是国家的根本。君主对待民众，绝不可轻忽，更不能欺压，而应当尽力地爱护和保护。

60. To the people the ruler is like their heart; to the ruler the people are like his body

Confucius remarked, "To the people the ruler is as their heart; to the ruler the people are as his body. ... The heart is safe if the body is complete and secure; and a wound in the body also makes the heart suffer. So the ruler is preserved by the people, and perishes also through the people.

Book of Rituals · Black Robes

【 Commentary 】

This is a perfect analogy. The ruler is likened to a heart and the people are likened to the body. Whether the heart will be preserved or not depends on the state of the body. The ruler should be aware of the fact that the people are the roots of a state, and he should do the utmost to protect and love the people instead of neglecting or oppressing them.

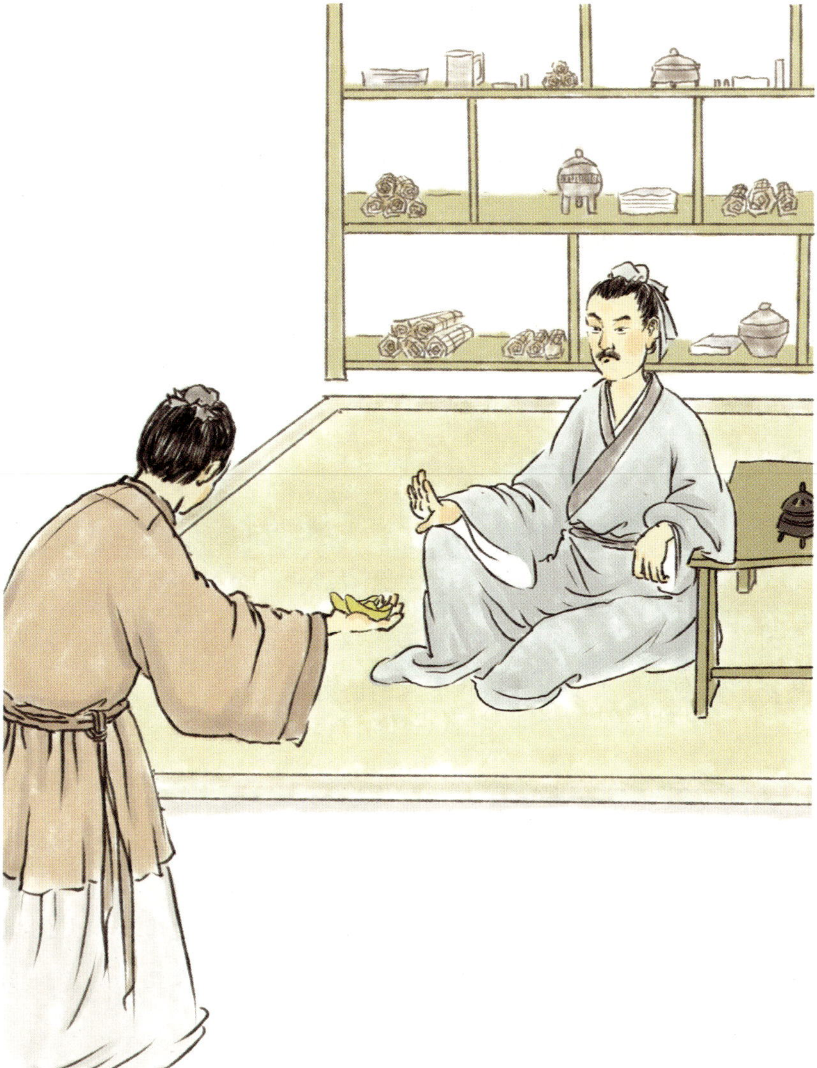

61. 忠信以为宝

【原文】

儒有不宝金玉，而忠信以为宝。不祈土地，立义以为土地。不祈多积，多文以为富。

《礼记·儒行》

【释文】

儒者不把金玉看成宝，而把忠信看成宝。他们不祈求土地，而是树立起道义作为他们安身立命的土地。他们不祈求多积财富，而是把尽量多地积累文化知识作为他们的财富。

【解析】

古人认为，儒者（后世泛指读书人）应注重道德修养和文化知识积累，注重独立人格的树立，把精神上的追求放在物质利益的追求之上。

61.The scholar considers loyalty and good faith as precious treasures

The scholar does not consider gold and jade as precious treasures, but loyalty and good faith; he does not desire lands, but considers the establishment of honor and duty as his domain; he does not desire a great accumulation of wealth, but considers the acquisition of abundant knowledge as his fortune.

Book of Rituals · The Conduct of a Scholar

【 Commentary 】

A scholar should lay stress on the cultivation of moral beings, the accumulation of knowledge, and the establishment of independent character. His spiritual pursuit should be prioritized over the pursuit of wealth.

62. 儒者之刚毅

儒有可亲而不可劫也，可近而不可迫也，可杀而不可辱也。其居处不淫，其饮食不溽，其过失可微辨而不可面数也。其刚毅有如此者。

《礼记·儒行》

【释文】

儒者可亲但不可以劫持他，可近但不可以威胁他，甚至可以杀他但不可以羞辱他。儒者的住处不追求奢侈，儒者的饮食不讲究丰厚，儒者的过失可以委婉地批评但不可以当面斥责。儒者的刚毅有的就像这样。

【解析】

儒者认为自身具有浩然正气，站在道德的制高点，因此刚毅果敢，面对威势也不屈服，宁死也不受辱。

62. The boldness and determination of the scholar

Close relations may be cultivated with the scholar, but no attempt must be made to constrain him; friendly association can be sought with him, but cannot be forced on him; he may be killed, but cannot be humiliated; he will not be extravagant in his dwelling; he will not be luxurious in eating and drinking; he may be gently admonished of his errors and failures, but he should not enumerate them before him — such is the boldness and determination of the scholar.

Book of Rituals · The Conduct of a Scholar

【 Commentary 】

With a noble spirit, a scholar is brave and decisive for he occupies the high moral ground. He will never yield to the authority, nor will he accept humiliation even at the expense of his life.

63. 儒者之忧思

【原文】

儒有今人与居，古人与稽；今世行之，后世以为楷；适弗逢世，上弗援，下弗推，谗谄之民有比党而危之者，身可危也，而志不可夺也；虽危起居，竟信其志，犹将不忘百姓之病也。其忧思有如此者。

《礼记·儒行》

【释文】

儒者虽然和当代的人生活在一起，但他却能稽考效法古代君子的言行；他现在的言行，后世将奉为楷模。他生不逢时，上面的人不援用他，下面的人也不推举他，那些造谣中伤逢迎巴结的人还要勾结起来陷害他。但这只能损伤他的身体，却绝对改变不了他的志向。虽然处境险恶，但他还一心想着施展自己的抱负，还念念不忘民众的痛苦。儒者的忧民意识有的就像这样。

【解析】

儒者一般都有强烈的历史使命感和高度的社会责任感，他们往往把施行仁政，救民于水火，使天下太平，作为自己的历史责任和神圣使命。

63.The anxiety that a scholar cherishes

The scholar lives with men of the present day, but the men of antiquity are the subjects of his study. Following their principles in the present age, he will become a model in future ages. If it should be that his own age does not understand him, that those above him do not promote him, and those below him do not support him, or even that calumniators and flatterers band together to put him in danger, his person may be placed in peril, but his aspiration cannot be taken out of him. Though danger may threaten him wherever he is, he will still pursue his aim, and never forget the afflictions of the people — such is the anxiety which he cherishes.

Book of Rituals · The Conduct of a Scholar

【 Commentary 】

A scholar has a strong sense of historical and social responsibility. A scholar will carry out the policy of humanity, save the people from affliction, and further the cause of peace in the world.

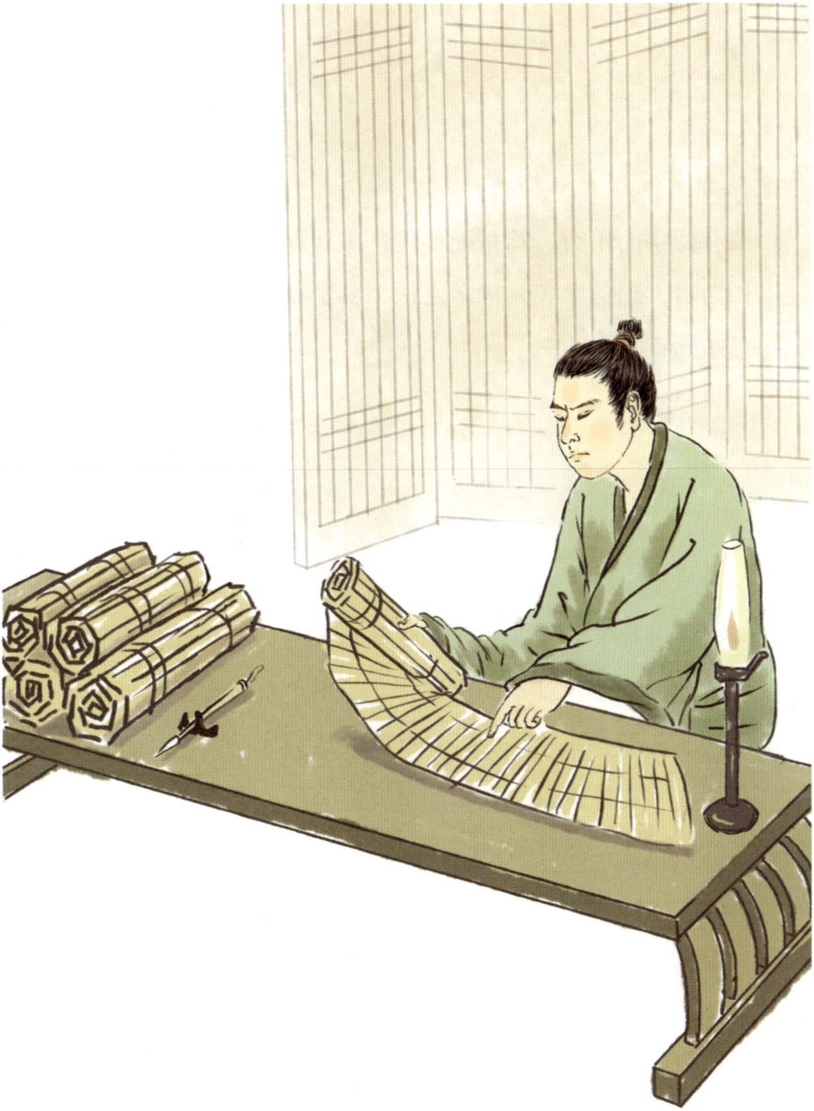

64. 儒者之宽裕

【原文】

儒有博学而不穷，笃行而不倦，幽居而不淫，上通而不困，礼之以和为贵，忠信之美，优游之法，慕贤而容众，毁方而瓦合。其宽裕有如此者。

《礼记·儒行》

【释文】

儒者广博地学习而不停步，认真地实行而不厌倦，隐居独处时不做坏事，通达为政时不会困窘，礼的运用以和为贵，推崇忠信的美德，效法从容和顺的风度，仰慕贤人又能容纳众人，放弃自己高傲的矜持而与如瓦器般的大众相融合。儒者的胸襟宽阔而能容众有的就像这样。

【解析】

儒者总能一方面严于律己，另一方面则宽以待人。其为人忠厚，胸襟宽阔，重团结，能包容。

64. The largeness and generosity of a scholar's spirit

The scholar learns extensively, but never allows his researches to come to an end; he does what he does with all his might, but is never weary; he may be living solitarily, but does not give way to licentiousness; he may be having free course in his acknowledged position, but is not hampered by it; in his practice of rituals he shows the value which he sets on harmony; in the excellence of his loyalty and good faith, he acts under the law of a benignant playfulness; he admires for virtuous and able men, and yet is forbearing and kind to all; he is like a potter who breaks his square mould, and his tiles are found to fit together — such is the largeness and generosity of his spirit.

Book of Rituals · The Conduct of a Scholar

【 Commentary 】

A scholar is extremely strict with himself, but is lenient with others. A scholar is loyal, kind, generous and tolerant.

65. 儒者之举贤援能

【原文】

　　儒有内称不辟亲，外举不辟怨。程功积事，推贤而进达之。不望其报，君得其志；苟利国家，不求富贵。其举贤援能有如此者。

《礼记·儒行》

【释文】

　　儒者举荐贤才，不有意回避宗族内的亲人，也不有意避开宗族外的仇人。他只根据其人的亲身经历和立功表现，把贤能之人举荐出来供朝廷任用。他不求回报，而只求满足君主的心意；他只求有利于国家，而不求自身的富贵。儒者的举荐贤才有的就像这样。

【解析】

　　儒者举荐贤才，完全是出以公心而不是谋取私利，只考虑国家利益而不计较个人得失。

65.Promoting the employment of the worthy and brining forward the talented

The scholar recommends members of his own family to public employment, without shrinking from doing so, and proposes others, without regard to their being at enmity with him. He takes into consideration all their merits and services, selecting those of virtue and ability, and putting them forward, without expecting any recompense from them; the ruler thus gets what he wishes, and if benefit results to the state, the scholar does not seek wealth or honors for himself — such is he in promoting the employment of the worthy and bringing forward the talented.

Book of Rituals · The Conduct of a Scholar

【 Commentary 】

A scholar will recommend the talented and worthy people for the public good, not for his private interest. He will put the interest of the state before his personal gains.

66. 儒者之尊让

温良者，仁之本也；敬慎者，仁之地也；宽裕者，仁之作也；孙接者，仁之能也；礼节者，仁之貌也；言谈者，仁之文也；歌乐者，仁之和也；分散者，仁之施也。儒皆兼此而有之，犹且不敢言仁也。其尊让有如此者。

《礼记·儒行》

温柔善良，是仁者的本性；恭敬谨慎，是仁者的资质；胸襟广阔，是仁者的气度；谦逊待人，是仁者的能力；礼仪合度，是仁者的外表；侃侃而谈，是仁者的文采；音乐弹唱，是仁者的亲和；分散财物，是仁者的布施。儒者具备了上述的种种美德，还是不敢说自己是仁人。儒者的恭敬谦让有的就像这样。

孔子思想的核心是仁。仁的内涵极广，涵盖了孝悌忠恕、爱国爱民、礼义廉耻、诚实守信等许多内容，恭敬谦让仅是其中之一。儒者终身都在努力，以求不断完善自己的仁德。

66.The humility of a scholar

Gentleness and goodness are the basics of humanity; respect and attention are the ground on which it stands; generosity and large-mindedness are the manifestation of it; humility and courtesy are the ability of it; ceremonial rules are the demonstration of it; speech is the ornament of it; singing and music are the harmony of it; sharing and distribution are the giving of it. The scholar possesses all these qualities in union, but he will not venture to claim a perfect humanity — such is the humility with which he declines it for himself.

Book of Rituals · The Conduct of a Scholar

【 Commentary 】

The core of Confucianism is humanity. It is very rich in content: filial piety, respect, loyalty, tolerance, patriotism, honor, duty, sincerity, trustfulness, etc. Without a doubt, being reverential and showing respects for others are included. A true Confucian scholar will exert lifelong efforts in elevating his moral standards.

67. 何故曰儒

儒有不陨获于贫贱，不充诎于富贵，不愿君王，不累长上，不闵有司，故曰儒。

《礼记·儒行》

儒者不因贫贱而丧失志向，不因富贵而丧失节操，不因为国君的辱骂、长上的钳制、官吏的诬蔑刁难而去做违背道义的事，所以才叫作"儒"。

儒者在任何时候，都应保持高尚的操守和独立的人格。贫贱不失志，富贵不淫乱，在权威高压之下也不低头屈服。

67.The styles of a true scholar

The scholar will not be cast down by poverty and mean condition. He will be not elated or exhausted by riches and noble condition. He will feel no disgrace that rulers and kings may try to inflict. He will be above the bonds that elders and superiors may try to impose. Superior officers cannot distress him. Therefore, he is styled a scholar.

Book of Rituals · The Conduct of a Scholar

【 Commentary 】

A true Confucian scholar will always maintain his moral standards and integrity. He will not swerve from his principles when poverty and mean condition strikes, nor will he yield to any temptation of riches and honors, or force from the authority.

68. 大学"三纲领"

【原文】

大学之道，在明明德，在亲民，在止于至善。

《礼记·大学》

【释文】

大学的宗旨在于使学者彰显光明的德性，在于使学者弃旧图新，在于使学者努力追求并最终达到最完善的道德境界。

【解析】

大学的宗旨这三句话，被称作大学的"三纲领"，其实质是为了使学者完善人格，"精神成人"。与功利性的"专业成才"相比，培养健全人格的"精神成人"更为重要。

68."Three Guidelines" of Higher Education

The object of a Higher Education is to bring out the intelligent moral power of our nature; to make a new and better society; and to enable us to abide in the highest excellence.

Book of Rituals · Higher Education

【 Commentary 】

These lines, known as the "Three Guidelines" of Higher Education, are essential for the intellectuals to cultivate and perfect their character, because "reaching spiritual adulthood" is even more important than the utilitarian pursuit of "becoming a professional in career."

69. 大学"八条目"

古之欲明明德于天下者，先治其国；欲治其国者，先齐其家；欲齐其家者，先修其身；欲修其身者，先正其心；欲正其心者，先诚其意；欲诚其意者，先致其知；致知在格物。

物格而后知至；知至而后意诚；意诚而后心正；心正而后身修；身修而后家齐；家齐而后国治；国治而后天下平。

《礼记·大学》

【释文】

古代那些要想在天下彰显光明德性从而平治天下的人，先要治理好自己的国家；要想治理好自己的国家，先要整治好自己的家庭；要想整治好自己的家庭，先要修养好自身的品性；要想修养好自身的品性，先要端正好自己的心思；要想端正好自己的心思，先要使自己的意念真诚；要想使自己的意念真诚，先要使自己获得知识；获得知识的途径在于接触和研究万事万物。

通过对万事万物的接触和研究之后才能获得知识；获得知识之后意念才能真诚；意念真诚之后心思才能端正；心思端正之后才能修养好自己的品性；自己的品性修养好之后才能整治好自己的家庭；整治好自己的家庭之后才能治理好国家；治理好国家之后才能去治理天下使天下太平。

69."Eight Particulars" of Higher Education

When ancient men wanted to further the cause of enlightenment and civilization in the world, they began first by securing good government in their country. To secure good government in their country, they began first by putting their house in order. To put their house in order, they began first by ordering their conversation aright. To put their conversation aright, they began first by putting their minds in a proper and well-ordered condition. To put their minds in a proper and well-ordered condition, they began first by getting true ideas. To have true ideas, they began first by acquiring knowledge and understanding. The acquirement of knowledge and understanding comes from a systematic study of things. After a systematic study of things, knowledge and understanding will come. When knowledge and understanding have come, men will have true ideas. When men have true ideas, their minds will be in a proper and well-ordered condition. When men's minds are in a proper and well-ordered condition, their conversation will be ordered aright. When men's conversations are ordered aright, their houses will be kept in order. When men's houses are kept in order, there will be good government. When there is good government in all countries, there will be peace and order in the world.

Book of Rituals · Higher Education

【解析】

这八句话是实现"三纲领"的"八条目",也可简化为:格物—致知—诚意—正心—修身—齐家—治国—平天下。(接触和研究万事万物——从学习和研究中广泛地获取知识——使自己的意念真诚——使自己的心思端正——修养好自己的品性——整治好自己的家庭——治理好国家——治理天下使天下太平。)

"三纲领""八条目",构成了一个完整的思想体系,千百年来,一直是许多人,许多知识分子,甚至许多平民百姓的执着追求,是他们的人生观、价值观的重要内容,是他们崇高的精神信仰。在"三纲领""八条目"熏陶之下,许多读书人都具有强烈的历史使命感和高度的社会责任感,认为"天下兴亡,匹夫有责"(天下国家的兴亡,每个人都有责任),将"以天下为己任"(使天下国家太平是自己的责任和使命)作为自己的人生信条。

【 Commentary 】

In order to fulfill the "Three Guidelines," later readers have extracted the "Eight Particulars" from the original texts, which should be carried out in this manner: A systematic study of things — Acquire knowledge and understanding — Get true ideas — Put the minds in a proper and well-ordered condition — Order the conversation aright — Put the house in order — Secure good government in the country — Further the cause of enlightenment and civilization in the world. Over thousands of years, this complete ideological system, consisting of the "Three Guidelines" and the "Eight Particulars," becomes a single-minded pursuit and sublime spiritual belief for many people, intellectuals and commoners alike. It dominates their outlook on life and value systems. As a result, a great many intellectuals have possessed a strong sense of historical mission and a high degree of social responsibility. And they believe in their lives that "all men share a common duty for the rise and the fall of a nation" and "it is the duty and mission of every man to further the cause of peace and development of a nation."

70. 修身为本

【原文】

自天子以至于庶人，壹是皆以修身为本。

《礼记·大学》

【释文】

上自天子，下至平民百姓，人人都要以修养自身品性为根本。

【解析】

在"八条目"中，"修身"为本，"修身"是最主要的条目，就好像一棵树，"修身"是它的根。"格物""致知""诚意""正心"，都是为了"修身"，是"培本"的功夫，好像水分和肥料，都是为了使根正苗壮。而"修身"，则是为今后成人成才苗壮成长奠定基础。因为只有在"修身"这个根基之上，才能进一步"齐家"（好像在根基上长成了粗壮的树干），才能进一步"治国""平天下"（好像大树长满了枝叶，绽开了鲜花），从而实现自己的理想与抱负。在大学求学，"修身"是根本，切不可本末倒置，更不可舍本逐末。

70.Order the conversation aright — the foundation

From the Emperor down to the lowest of the common people, the one thing that all must do is to make the ordering of their conversation aright, the foundation for everything.

Book of Rituals · Higher Education

【 Commentary 】

Among the "Eight Particulars," "ordering of the conversion aright" is the foundation for everything. And it can be likened to the root of a tree. "A systematic study of things," "acquire knowledge and understanding," "get true ideas," and "put the minds in a proper and well-ordered condition" are like water and fertilizer, without which the tree cannot take deep roots. Only when "ordering the conversation aright" is completed could "putting the house in order" (the tree trunk), "securing good government in the country" (branches), and "furthering the cause of enlightenment and civilization in the world" (flowers) be realized. Hence, one must not confuse the cause and the effect, for the "ordering of the conversation aright" is fundamental in fulfilling one's ideal and ambition.

71. 富润屋，德润身

【原文】

富润屋，德润身，心广体胖。故君子必诚其意。

《礼记·大学》

【释文】

财富可以装饰房屋，品德却可以修养身心，使心胸宽广而体态舒泰安详。所以，品德高尚的君子一定要使自己的意念真诚。

【解析】

人们往往重视"富润屋"，轻忽"德润身"。但恰是后一句"德润身"，才更能彰显一个人的高贵与美丽。

71.Wealth embellishes a house, moral qualities embellish the person

Wealth embellishes a house, but moral qualities embellish the person. When the mind is free and easy, the body will grow in flesh. Therefore, a gentleman must have true ideas.

Book of Rituals · Higher Education

【 Commentary 】

We are used to overemphasizing the fact that "wealth embellishes a house," and ignoring the truth that "moral qualities embellish the person." Yet a person's moral qualities can best demonstrate his or her nobility and beauty.

72. 明明德

　　《康诰》曰："克明德。"《大甲》曰："顾诶天之明命。"《帝典》曰："克明峻德。"皆自明也。

《礼记·大学》

【释文】

　　《尚书·周书·康诰》说："能够彰显光明的德性。"《尚书·商书·太甲》说："要重视这上天赋予的光明禀性。"《尚书·虞夏书·尧典》说："能够彰显崇高的德性。"这些都是说要自己彰显光明而崇高的德性。

【解析】

　　"三纲领"的第一条就是"明明德"（彰显光明的德性）。周初执政者很重视"德"。殷与周，在政治思想观念上有很大不同，简言之，殷商"尊天事鬼"，而周则"敬德保民"。周初的执政者认为，周王朝是靠"德"取得天下，也应靠"德"保有天下。"皆自明也"强调的是个体的主观精神，指明了要获得光明美好的道德，主要依靠自己的努力。

72.Bring out the intelligent moral power of our nature

The Commission of Investiture to Prince Kang says: "He (the Emperor Wen) succeeded in making manifest the power of his moral nature." In the *Address of the Minister I Yin to the Emperor Tai Jia*, it is said, "He (the great Emperor Tang) kept constantly before him the clear Ordinance of God." In the *Memorial Record of the Emperor Yao*, it is said, "He succeeded in making manifest the lofty sublimity of his moral nature." Thus all these men made manifest the intelligent moral power of their nature.

Book of Rituals · Higher Education

【 Commentary 】

The first "Guideline" is "to bring out the intelligent moral power of our nature." During the early period of Zhou Dynasty, its rulers put a high value on "moral nature." The two dynasties, Yin and Zhou, varied a great deal in political thoughts: the former "respects the heaven and worships the ghosts," whereas the latter "values the moral nature and nurtures the people." The Zhou people deemed that it was the "moral nature" that helped them attain and thereupon sustain sovereignty. The last sentence highlights the fact that to acquire the intelligent moral power of nature depends mainly on spiritual strength and individual efforts.

73. 日新又新

苟日新，日日新，又日新。

《礼记·大学》

如果能够一天更新，就应天天更新，更新了还要再更新。

这是汤之《盘铭》上的三句话。汤是殷商王朝开国之君，这三句话说明当一个王朝刚建立的时候，执政者总是力图除旧更新的。今天在大学求学的人，也应以此为座右铭，努力地不断地革故鼎新，弃旧图新，革除旧我，获得新生。

73.Be new from day to day and everyday

Be a new man each day; from day to day, be a new man; every day, be a new man.

Book of Rituals · Higher Education

【 Commentary 】

This line was taken from *The Inscription on the Emperor Tang's Bath*. Tang was the first Emperor of the Yin Shang Dynasty. While establishing a new regime, the rulers strive for exchanging the old for the new. Those who seek knowledge in Higher Education should take this line as a motto. Only by forsaking the past and starting afresh could the self-regeneration be accomplished.

74. 其命维新

周虽旧邦，其命惟新。

《礼记·大学》

【释文】

周王朝虽然是旧的邦国，但却禀受了新的天命。

【解析】

"三纲领"的第二条就是"亲民"（使人弃旧图新）。武王革命，推翻了商纣王，建立了周王朝。新王朝力图除旧更新：个人有新的道德，社会有新的风气，政治有新的举措，国家有新的面貌，整个社会欣欣向荣。

74. A new mission was given

Royal House of Zhou was an old State, a new mission was given to it.

Book of Rituals · Higher Education

【 Commentary 】

The second "Guideline" is "to make a new and better society" (forsake the past and start afresh). The revolution started by the Emperor Wu overthrew the ruling of the Emperor Zhou of Shang Dynasty, and helped the former establish the Zhou Dynasty. This guideline applies naturally to a new dynasty: for the individuals, there will be new moral standards; the society, new ethos; the politics, new measures; the nation, new looks; and a scene of prosperity will spread out through the whole society.

75. 知其所止

【原文】

于止，知其所止，可以人而不如鸟乎！

《礼记·大学》

【释文】

谈到居止，人就应当知道自己的归宿。连黄鸟都知道它该栖息在什么地方，难道人还可以不如一只鸟儿吗？

【解析】

"止"意为"居止"，是人们要到达并留居的地方。正如民有住房、鸟有归巢一样，作为毕生安身立命之所，每一个人也应当有精神上的追求，寻求最终的精神归宿。这种精神追求，其实就是信仰。"三纲领"的第三条明确提出，学者应"止于至善"，就是要将"至善"作为精神信仰并终身追求。

75.Know what to choose for the abode

In choosing their abode, even the birds know what to choose. Can it be that man is less intelligent than birds?

Book of Rituals · Higher Education

【 Commentary 】

A bird flies back to its nest and a person returns home. Likewise, each and every person should seek an ultimate spiritual home, where his soul could be entrusted. This spiritual pursuit matches the third "Guideline" that a scholar must "abide in the highest excellence," and it should be the faith that scholars maintain in their lifelong efforts.

76. 止于至善

【原文】

　　为人君，止于仁；为人臣，止于敬；为人子，止于孝；为人父，止于慈；与国人交，止于信。

《礼记·大学》

【释文】

　　作为国君，要做到仁爱；作为臣子，要做到恭敬；作为子女，要做到孝顺；作为父亲，要做到慈爱；与国人交往，要做到诚信。

76.Abide in the highest excellence

As a ruler, his ideal was to love mankind. As a subject, his ideal was to respect authority. As a son his ideal was to be a dutiful son. As a father, his ideal was to be kind to his children. In intercourse with his fellow men, his ideal was to be faithful and true.

Book of Rituals · Higher Education

【 Commentary 】

The "highest excellence" means the "best" and "extreme goodness." It refers to the highest level of moral state. Specifically, this entry shows us that "humanity," "respects," "filial piety," "kindness" and "trust" are all included in this "highest excellence." Equally important are the political ethics and moral integrity of men in authority, such as "promoting the talents," "respecting the relatives," "bring happiness and benefits to people," etc. In Han Dynasty, "humanity," "honor and duty," "rituals," "intelligence" and "trust" were regarded as the "Five Moral Qualities." Nowadays, they are as important as daily necessities, without which we could not live even for one moment. "Humanity": A moral man loves all human beings. He loves his parents and seniors, his brothers and sisters, his friends and other strangers. He loves the general public, the nation, the nature and the earth on

【解析】

　　"至善"就是"最好""极好"，指道德最崇高的境界。这里揭示了"至善"的具体内容，包括"仁""敬""孝""慈""信"。此外还包括执政者的政治伦理与道德操守，如"贤贤""亲亲"与"乐民""利民"，等等。汉代以"仁""义""礼""智""信"为"五常"。今天，"五常"对于我们，也同布帛菽粟一样，是不可须臾离的东西：仁——仁者爱人，仁的意思爱人，是要爱父母长辈，爱兄弟姐妹，进而爱朋友，爱他人，爱民众，爱国家，爱大自然，爱我们人类赖以生存的家园。义——义者宜也，义的意思是适宜、恰当，做事要恰当合理，讲道义，求真理，走正道，坚守公平正义。礼——礼即礼法制度，以及与之相适应的礼仪、礼俗、礼貌，在日常生活中，要讲文明，有礼貌，以礼待人，遵纪守法。智——智是智慧，重在明辨是非，分清善恶，从而决定取舍。信——信是诚实守信，表里如一，言行一致，重然诺，讲信用，言必信，行必果，有诚意，无二心，待人忠诚，不搞欺蒙诈骗。两千年来，仁、义、礼、智、信这"五常"成了中国人主要的精神追求与道德规范，是中国人不可摧毁的精神信仰。仁、义、礼、智、信实为中华民族优秀文化传统的核心与精髓。

which we are dwelling. "Honor and duty" denote a sense of appropriateness, and imply that one needs to take the apposite and appropriate measures in doing everything, especially in the pursuit of truth. One also must maintain the principles of fairness and justice. "Ritual" means the ceremonial rituals, proprieties, and usages of social life. One should be civil, treat others politely and obey the rules and regulations. "Intelligence": It is important to be able to tell right from wrong, and be clear about what is good and what is evil, so as to make the correct decision. "Trust" means being honest and truthful. What one says and does should correspond with what is on one's mind. One must be true in word and resolute in deed. One also should treat people sincerely and never deceive others. Over two thousand years, these "Five Moral Qualities" have become the predominant spiritual ideals, moral norms as well as the unswerving faith for Chinese people. They represent the core values of Chinese culture and traditions.

77. 一家仁，一国兴仁

【原文】

　　一家仁，一国兴仁；一家让，一国兴让；一人贪戾，一国作乱。其机如此。此谓一言偾事，一人定国。

《礼记·大学》

【释文】

　　如果一家是仁爱的，一国也会兴起仁爱之风；如果一家是礼让的，一国也会兴起礼让之风；如果有一人贪婪暴戾，一国就会发生动乱。其先兆就是这样清楚。这就叫作说错一句话就会使事情败坏，端正一个人就能使国家安定。

【解析】

　　"家风"会影响"国风"。在上位的人的所作所为往往对家庭和国家造成很大的甚至是决定性的影响。

77.Kindness and humanity in one family, the whole nation grows kind and humane

When there is kindness and humanity in one family, the whole nation will grow kind and humane. When there is courtesy and politeness in one family, the whole nation will all become polite and courteous. The ambition and perversity of one man, on the other hand, may bring confusion and anarchy to the whole nation. Such is the power of influence. Hence the saying: "One word can ruin everything; one man can save a nation."

Book of Rituals · Higher Education

【 Commentary 】

The "ethos of a family" will affect the "ethos of a nation." More often than not, what those in authority do and how they behave will exercise a strong, sometimes decisive, influence upon the family and the society.

78. 得众则得国，失众则失国

【原文】

道得众则得国，失众则失国。

《礼记·大学》

【释文】

国君有道，得到民心就能得到国家；国君无道，失去民心就会失去国家。

【解析】

战国时期思想家荀子曾说，国君像船，人民像水，水可以把船浮起来，也可以把船掀翻。

78. When a ruler gains the hearts of the people, he will gain the kingdom

When a ruler gains the hearts of the people, he will gain the kingdom; when he loses the hearts of the people, he will lose the kingdom.

Book of Rituals · Higher Education

【 Commentary 】

An ancient Chinese philosopher Xunzi (313-238 B.C.) once commented, a ruler can be likened to a boat, and people the water. A boat can float on the water, yet the waves can also turn the boat upside down.

79. 德本财末

【原文】

德者，本也；财者，末也。

《礼记·大学》

【释文】

品德啊，这是根本；财富啊，这是枝末。

【解析】

在上位的人要分清本末，不可本末倒置。应将修养品德视为根本，放在首位，切不可见利忘义，疯狂敛财。

79.Moral quality, the foundation; wealth, the means

Moral qualities are the foundation of a nation. Wealth is but the means.

Book of Rituals · Higher Education

【 Commentary 】

Those in authority must not put the cart before the horse. The cultivation of moral character and the foundation of a nation should be prioritized. It is wrong to accumulate wealth in an unrestricted and unscrupulous manner.

80. 财散民聚

财聚则民散，财散则民聚。

《礼记·大学》

【释文】

国君聚敛财富民心就会离散，国君散财于民民心就会凝聚。

【解析】

这是一条重要的历史经验，也是一个颠扑不破的真理。

80.The distribution of wealth among the many contributes to the stability of society

The accumulation of wealth in a few hands leads to the dissolution of society, while the distribution of wealth among the many contributes to the stability of society.

Book of Rituals · Higher Education

【 Commentary 】

This is a significant experience from history as well as an irrefutable truth.

81. 仁者以财发身，不仁者以身发财

【原文】

仁者以财发身，不仁者以身发财。未有上好仁而下不好义者也，未有好义其事不终者也，未有府库财非其财者也。

《礼记·大学》

【释文】

仁爱的人仗义疏财以成名起家，不仁的人不惜以生命为代价去敛钱发财。没有在上位的人喜好仁德而在下位的人却不喜好忠义的，没有喜好忠义而为国君做事却半途而废的，没有不将府库里的财物当成自己财物而加以保护的。

【解析】

孔子对"义"和"利"，有着非常辩证的看法。他认为居上位的"君子"，如果为谋一己之私利而抛弃道义，就会遭致民众的怨恨。君子应该根据道义去"利民"，这样一来就会得到民众的拥护，这就叫作"以义为利"。长期以来，儒家都十分重视公私之分、义利之辨，认为这是修身和从政一个重要的原则问题。

81.Moral men make money to live; immoral men live to make money

Moral men make money to live. Immoral men live to make money. You will never find where the rulers are human and kind that the people do not love honor and duty. You will never find where the people in a nation love honor and duty, that the affairs of that nation do not prosper, and that the wealth in the nation does not belong to the ruler.

Book of Rituals · Higher Education

【 Commentary 】

Confucius maintained a dialectic view towards the "moral qualities" and the "wealth." In particular, he advised the "moral men" in authority: bring benefits to the people and they will return their respect and support; whereas exploiting one's position for personal gains at the expense of honor and duty will only invite resentment from the people. And that is why "honor and duty make a nation prosperous." The Confucian scholars have always kept in mind the dividing line between the public and the private, between the moral qualities and the material properties, for it is essential for self-cultivation and political governance.

82. 以义为利

国不以利为利，以义为利也。

《礼记·大学》

【释文】

治理一个国家的君主不应该以财货为利益，而应该以仁义为利益。

【解析】

在上位的人不应聚敛财富，谋取私利，而应施行仁义，造福社会和人民。

82.Honor and duty make a nation prosperous

What really makes a nation prosperous is not wealth and material prosperity, but honor and duty.

Book of Rituals · Higher Education

【 Commentary 】

Those in authority should not accumulate the wealth for personal gains, but bring benefits, in accordance with honor and duty, to the society and the people.

83. 成人礼

【原文】

    成人之者，将责成人礼焉也。责成人礼焉者，将责为人子、为人弟、为人臣、为人少者之礼行焉。将责四者之行于人，其礼可不重与！

《礼记·冠义》

【释文】

    既然已经成人，那就要用成人礼来要求他。所谓用成人礼来要求他，就是要求他按照做儿子、做弟弟、做臣子、做后辈应守的礼来行事。要求他对待父母、兄长、国君、长辈都要依礼而行，这样说来对冠礼能不重视吗！

【解析】

    古代男子，二十岁算是成人，要举行成人礼，也就是加冠礼，在仪式上要束发加冠。成人礼后，就要求他用成人的礼节来行事。这不仅是礼节礼貌上的要求，更是内心道德情操的养成。也就是让他通过践行成人的礼节，从而培养起孝敬父母、尊敬长辈、顺从长上、忠于国君的道德情操，不断增强修身、齐家、治国、平天下的社会责任感。

83.Rituals on Reaching Adulthood

Those who reach their adulthood will be required all the observances of an adult. They will be required to perform the duties of a son, a younger brother, a subject and a junior. Since all these four duties will be entrusted to them, how could the rituals not to be considered important?

Book of Rituals · The Meaning of Capping Rituals

【 Commentary 】

In ancient China, a twenty-year-old man was regarded as an adult, and there would be a "Capping Ceremony" for him. On his "coming of age" day, a man would be capped by the seniors. After the ceremony, he would have to act in according with the adult rituals. This was a requirement for his external manner and internal moral beings. The aim of the ceremonial process was to further elevate his moral standards, so that he would be more reverent in serving his parents and rulers. This would also strengthen the sense of his responsibility in self-cultivation, family issues and social matters.

84. 孝弟忠顺之行立，而后可以为人

【原文】

故孝弟忠顺之行立，而后可以为人；可以为人，而后可以治人也。

《礼记·冠义》

【释文】

因此一个人做到了对父母孝敬，对兄长友爱，对国君忠诚，对长辈顺从，然后才能被称为"成人"。能被称为"成人"的人，然后才可以从政，去治理别人。

【解析】

长大成人，最重要的事就是按照成人的道德标准来修身，譬如孝悌忠信、礼义廉耻，等等，都是必须做到的。只有在修身的基础上，才可以走上政坛，从事政务活动。

84.Only when his practice of filial and fraternal duties, of political loyalty and deferential submission is established could he be regarded as an adult

Therefore, only when his practice of filial and fraternal duties, of political loyalty and deferential submission is established could he be regarded as an adult. Only when he could be regarded as an adult could he be qualified to govern others.

Book of Rituals · The Meaning of Capping Rituals

【 Commentary 】

The fundamental thing for an adult to do is to perfect oneself according to the moral standards in the adult world. He must be filial, loyal, respectful, and sincere. He must know honors and duties. Self-cultivation will lay a solid foundation for future success in political career.

85. 昏礼者，将合二姓之好

【原文】

　　昏礼者，将合二姓之好，上以事宗庙，而下以继后世也，故君子重之。

《礼记·昏义》

【释文】

　　婚礼，是一种加强两姓之间的亲密关系、上能延续宗庙祭祀、下能繁衍子孙后代的礼仪，所以君子很重视它。

【解析】

　　古代实行同姓不婚，贵族成年男子往往迎娶别的诸侯国异姓女子为妻。古代婚礼十分隆重，而且有一定的程序，称为"六礼"，这就是纳采（遣媒提亲）、问名（询问女名）、纳吉（通报卜吉）、纳征（赠送聘礼）、请期（商定婚期）、亲迎（男子亲迎）。古代贵族之所以重视婚礼，主要是因为他们认为成年男女结成婚姻，才有后嗣，才能延续宗庙祭祀，从而使国家稳定，国运长久。

85.The ceremony of marriage was intended to be a bond of love between two different families

The ceremony of marriage was intended to be a bond of love between two different families, with a view to secure the services in the ancestral temple and the continuance of the family line. Therefore, moral men set a great value upon it.

Book of Rituals · The Meaning of Marriage

【 Commentary 】

In ancient China, two families with the same surname are disallowed to tie a marital bond. A male adult will usually marry a female of a different surname from a distant place. A grand wedding ceremony include "Six Steps": 1) sending a matchmaker for the engagement, 2) requesting the name of the bride-to-be, 3) reporting the result of the divination of the name, 4) presenting gifts to the family of the bride-to-be, 5) calculating an auspicious day for the wedding, 6) going to the bride's home and escorting her to the wedding. The marriage is set with a great value, because the continuance of the family line resulted from the bond of a man and a woman will lay a solid foundation for a stable society and a prosperous country.

86. 昏礼者，礼之本也

【原文】

男女有别，而后夫妇有义；夫妇有义，而后父子有亲；父子有亲，而后君臣有正。故曰：昏礼者，礼之本也。

《礼记·昏义》

【释文】

男女有两性之别，然后才能结为夫妻而有夫妻之间的责任义务；有夫妻之间的责任义务，然后才能生儿育女而有父子之间的血缘亲情；有父子之间的血缘亲情，然后才能移孝作忠而有君臣之间的正常秩序。所以说，婚礼是各种礼的根本。

【解析】

古人认为，先有夫妻，然后才会有父子、君臣。因此，在各种社会关系中，最重视夫妻关系；在各种社会伦理道德中，最重视夫妻之间的伦理道德；而在各种礼仪中，则最重视婚礼。

86.The ceremony of marriage is the root of the other rituals

From the distinction between man and woman came the honor and duty between husband and wife. From that honor and duty came the affection between father and son. From that affection came the rectitude between ruler and subject. Whence it is said, "The ceremony of marriage is the root of other rituals."

Book of Rituals · The Meaning of Marriage

【 Commentary 】

In ancient China, the relation between husband and wife matters more than the relation between father and son, or the relationship between rule and subject. In various social associations, marital relation is set with a great value. Ethical rules in marital relation are more significant than all other moral standards. The ceremony of marriage is also the most important in the ritual system.

87. 妇顺者，顺于舅姑，和于室人

【原文】

　　妇顺者，顺于舅姑，和于室人，而后当于夫，以成丝麻布帛之事，以审守委积盖藏。是故妇顺备，而后内和理；内和理，而后家可长久也。故圣王重之。

《礼记·昏义》

【释文】

　　所谓妇的顺从，首先是要对公婆顺从，与家人和睦，然后才能让丈夫满意，同时做好家庭妇女应做的养蚕缲丝、纺纱织布等事，并谨慎地保管好家中的财物。所以说，上述对妇顺的要求都做到了，家庭内部才能和谐安定；家庭内部和谐安定了，家业才能长久兴旺。因此圣明的君主都很重视妇顺。

【解析】

　　中国古代社会的构成，以家庭为基本细胞。家庭稳定和谐，国家才能稳定安宁。而在传统的"男主外，女主内"的家庭模式中，家庭内部的稳定和谐，家庭主妇自然负有主要的责任。因此孝顺公婆，团结家人，配合丈夫，勤俭持家，就成了对家庭主妇的必然要求。

87.When the wife was deferential, she was obedient to her parents-in-law and harmonious with all other family members

When the wife was deferential, she was obedient to her parents-in-law and harmonious with all other family members. She was the fitting partner of her husband and could carry on all the work in silk and linen, making cloth and silken fabrics, and maintaining a watchful care over the various stores and depositories of the household. In this way when the deferential obedience of the wife was complete, the internal harmony was secured; and when the internal harmony was secured, the long continuance of the family could be expected. Therefore, the ancient kings attached great importance to the marriage ceremonies.

Book of Rituals · The Meaning of Marriage

【 Commentary 】

In ancient China, family was the basic unit in the society. When a harmonious family is secured, a stable and peaceful country is expected. The mode that an ancient Chinese family maintained was that men would work outside home and women would manage the family issues. Hence, the housewife was responsible for the stability and harmony of a family. She was required to be obedient to her parents-in-law and harmonious with all other family members. She must also be the fitting partner of her husband, and thriftily manage the whole family.

88. 妇之四德

【原文】

教以妇德、妇言、妇容、妇功。

《礼记·昏义》

【释文】

在女子出嫁之前，要教她知道主妇的德行、言辞、仪容、女工。

【解析】

古代贵族女子，在出嫁之前的三个月，要在祖庙里由长辈教她知道出嫁后怎样做一个家庭主妇。所教内容主要有四方面：德行，主要是对公婆、丈夫顺从，使家庭和睦；言辞，主要是谈吐文明有礼；仪容，主要是仪表端庄，面容恭顺；女工，主要指家庭妇女应做的养蚕缫丝、纺纱织布等事。这些都是对一个家庭主妇的必然要求，后来也成为所有成年女子提高文明修养的主要内容。

88.Four moral characters of a wife

She was taught the virtue, the speech, the manner, and the work of a wife.

Book of Rituals · The Meaning of Marriage

【 Commentary 】

In ancient China, a bride-to-be would stay in the ancestor temple and study how to become a qualified housewife with senior family members. She would study what were related to the following four aspects: 1) the virtue: be obedient to her parents-in-law and husband, and maintain a harmonious family; 2) the speech: be courteous and use tactful language; 3) the manner: it mainly refers to the decent and graceful appearance and reverential attitude; 4) the work: the work in silk and linen, making cloth and silken fabrics, and maintaining a watchful care over the various stores and depositories of the household, etc. These were all the requirements for a housewife, and for elevating the moral standards of adult women.

89. 君子比德于玉

夫昔者君子比德于玉焉：温润而泽，仁也；缜密以栗，知也；廉而不刿，义也；垂之如队，礼也；叩之其声清越以长，其终诎然，乐也；瑕不掩瑜，瑜不掩瑕，忠也；孚尹旁达，信也；气如白虹，天也；精神见于山川，地也；圭璋特达，德也；天下莫不贵者，道也。《诗》云："言念君子，温其如玉。"故君子贵之也。

《礼记·聘义》

从前的君子，用玉来比喻和象征人的德行：玉温和而又润泽，像仁；缜密而又纹理清晰，像智；有棱角但不伤人，像义；玉佩垂而下坠，像礼；轻轻一击其声清扬悠长，最后又戛然而止，像乐；纯净不掩盖其瑕疵，瑕疵也不掩盖其纯净，像忠；色彩外露而不隐蔽，像信；宝玉之上光耀如白虹，像天；产玉之所山川草木润泽不枯，像地；朝聘时凭内在充实的美可以直接奉呈，像德；普天之下无人不看重玉的美德，像道。《诗经·秦风·小戎》上说："多么想念君子啊，他的温润就像美玉。"所以君子看重玉。

89.Ancient moral men found the likeness of all excellent qualities in jade

Ancient moral men found the likeness of all excellent qualities in jade. Soft, smooth, and glossy, it appeared to them like humanity; fine, compact, and strong — like intelligence; angular, but not sharp and cutting — like honor and duty; hanging down in beads as if it would fall — like the humility of rituals; when struck, yielding a note, clear and prolonged, yet terminating abruptly — like music; its flaws not concealing its beauty, nor its beauty concealing its flaws — like loyalty; with an internal radiance issuing from it on every side — like good faith; bright as a brilliant rainbow — like the heaven; exquisite and mysterious, appearing in the hills and streams — like the earth; standing out conspicuous in the symbols of rank — like moral beings; esteemed by all under the heaven — like the great Way. In the *Book of Poetry*, it is said that "He rises in my mind, lovely and bland, like jade of the richest kind."

Book of Rituals · The Meaning of the Interchange of Missions between

Different Courts

【解析】

　　古人身上往往佩玉，含义深远。从修身来说，玉象征各种美德，佩玉可以勉励和鞭策自己，使道德不断完善。从外在仪表来说，佩玉在身，行走之时，铿锵有声，表示行止有节，彬彬有礼。此外，在古代聘礼和祭礼上，也往往用玉，玉是贵重的礼器。

【 Commentary 】

Ancient scholars often wore jade pieces. Jade is emblematic of various virtues, and it serves to encourage oneself and improve one's moral standards. It produces a clear and prolonged note when struck but the sound terminates abruptly. This will remind the scholar to act courteously and of his limits. Besides, in grand ceremony of marriage or sacrifice rituals, jade vessels were also widely used.

翻译后记

　　对于本书中所汇集的《大学》和《中庸》核心章节，英文翻译采用了辜鸿铭先生的版本，另外也对其部分译文做出了调整。其他《礼记》中的章节内容还分别参考了林语堂先生和理雅各的译本。同时要十分感谢广西师范大学出版社虞劲松老师、梁鑫磊老师、王专老师及其他匿名译审老师！没有他们的信任、支持和指导，这本译作是无法完成的。对于译文中的衍误和不妥之处，译者本人负全部责任。

吴思远

2018 年 12 月 30 日于北林海

༄ Postscripts ༅

For the English translation of the texts from *Daxue* (Higher Education) and *Zhongyong* (Central Harmony) in this present collection, I adopted a revised version of Gu Hongming's work. For the rest parts, I consulted Dr. Lin Yutang and James Legge's works. I would like to express my sincere gratitude to the editors of Guangxi Normal University Press: Mr. Yu Jingsong, Mr. Liang Xinlei, Ms. Wang Zhuan, and the anonymous proofreader. This book could not be completed without their trust, support and suggestions. For any errors remain in this book, I take complete responsibility for them.

Wu Siyuan

December 30, 2018

Bellingham, WA